The Healing Visit

Insights into the Mitzvah of Bikur Cholim

Bat Tova Zwebner & Chana Shofnos

TARGUM/FELDHEIM

First published 1989

ISBN 0-944070-17-5

Phototypeset at Targum Press

Printed in Israel

Published by:
Targum Press Inc.
22700 W. Eleven Mile Rd.
Southfield, Mich. 48034

Distributed by:
Philipp Feldheim Inc.
200 Airport Executive Park
Spring Valley, N.Y. 10977

Distributed in Israel by:
Nof Books Ltd.
POB 23646
Jerusalem 91235

The authors' proceeds from this book have been donated to bikur cholim causes.

*To my parents, Melvin and Zelda Tatel,
who raised us to meet life's challenges and
to serve others.*

Bat Tova Zwebner

*To my mother, Etta Willner, who spent
her share of time in hospitals visiting her
children and husband, and never lost her
faith in God, the One Who enables man
to rise above his limitations.*

*In memory of my father, Jack Willner, o"h,
whose understanding of human dignity
encouraged our family to live life to its
fullest potential.*

Chana Shofnos

Rabbi CHAIM P. SCHEINBERG

KIRYAT MATTERSDORF
PANIM MEIROT 2
JERUSALEM, ISRAEL

הרב חיים פנחס שיינברג
ראש ישיבת "תורה אור"
ומורה הוראה דקרית מטרסדורף
ירושלים טל. 536125

This book is a work of great importance.

The *mitzvah* of *bikur cholim* is recognized by all as one taught to us by the example of *HaShem Yisborach* Himself, *kavyachol*, when He came to visit *Avraham Avinu*.

But detailed knowledge of this *mitzvah* is sorely lacking. There are many who know the *halachos* but are unaware of the technicalities, and there are those who know the methods but not the Torah's guidance.

Chana Shofnos and Bat Tova Zwebner, who are instilled with *yiras shomayim*, and have the experience of much *nisayon*, wish to bring the understanding and "know-how" of this great *mitzvah* to all those who wish to keep it, to give support and encouragement to the sick.

They have spared no effort to complete their work, and have done so with the pure intention of helping those who wish to help others, and helping to make visitors' efforts worthwhile and successful.

May *HaShem* grant them the success this book deserves, and may it be received and acted upon by all.

Chaim Pinchus Scheinberg

RABBI S. WASSERMAN
PONIM MEIROT 15/10
MATERSDORF, JERUSALEM
ISRAEL (02) 537-420

הרב שמחה וסרמן
רח׳ פנים מאירות 15/10
מטרסדורף - ירושלים

Within the framework of today's universal *teshuvah* movement, Providence inspires a few individuals to call our attention to particular *mitzvos*. I congratulate Mrs. Chana Shofnos and Mrs. Bat Tova Zwebner, authors of *The Healing Visit*, who were *zocheh* to focus on the *mitzvah* of *bikur cholim*. May their efforts be blessed. We pray to the Almighty that He heal the pains of His people and bring its redemption about soon.

Rabbi Simcha Wasserman

shaare zedek medical center   מרכז רפואי שערי צדק

Dear Mrs. Shofnos and Mrs. Zwebner,

The *mitzvah* of *bikur cholim* cannot be overestimated. As Director-General of Shaare Zedek Medical Center, I am well aware of the psychological benefits to the patient when family and friends show in a practical way that they care and are concerned. Visiting the patient, whether an adult or a child, gives concrete expression to that concern and is an integral part of the healing process, as the patient feels the encouragement and the wish for his recovery.

The book that you have written with such sensitivity explains this in great detail. It also serves as a practical guide to *how* to visit a patient, and this is most important. Through research involving authorities—doctors, rabbis, social workers, nurses, etc.—it explains all the considerations surrounding visits to patients: the privacy that should be respected with regard to medical details; how long a visit should last; what should be brought to the hospital; when a visit should end; as well as practical ways to aid the patient during the convalescent period.

I wish you every success with this book and commend the valuable insights you have revealed through your in-depth research.

Sincerely,

J Haly

Jonathan Halevy, M.D.
Director-General

jerusalem 91-000 ירושלים
p.o.b. 293   293 .ת.נ
telephone 555-111 טלפון

Table of Contents

Foreword

The Torah ideal of doing acts of kindness stems from the sublime obligation to emulate the Almighty. Just as He is compassionate and merciful, so we must be compassionate and merciful. Visiting someone who is ill is an expression of this compassion. When we hear that someone is sick, the first thought that should enter our minds is, "What can I personally do to help this person?"

Unfortunately, many people hear that someone is ill but it does not motivate them to think in terms of practical action on their part. They might feel sorry for the person and for his relatives, but this can be just a fleeting sentiment, devoid of action. They fail to ask themselves the most crucial question, "What can I personally do?"

For some people this changes if they or someone very close to them become ill. Then they recognize firsthand the value of someone who sincerely cares. They appreciate what it means to have friends and acquaintances who are willing to do things for them.

This awareness can come about in a positive manner: they have seen models of people who have personified *chesed*. Or this might have been a painful lesson: people failed to come to their assistance. Loneliness, boredom, and difficult burdens were their teachers. Now they do not want others to experience the suffering they had.

The Healing Visit is a most needed addition to the growing Torah literature in English. The *mitzvah* of visiting the sick requires special sensitivity and awareness. It is so crucial to have a sense of what is appropriate to do and say and what one should avoid. Out of fear of making mistakes some people forgo many opportunities to do much *chesed*. Others might visit someone but fail to utilize their *chesed* potential. If they would only have realized that they could have done more than they did, they would gladly have done so.

When reading this book, keep asking yourself, "How can I apply these ideas?" Actually see yourself following through on what you read. When you picture yourself doing something, you are much likelier to carry it out in practice. At the very first opportunity to fulfill this *mitzvah*, do something concrete to integrate what you have read. There is a major difference between just reading about an important idea, and reading a handbook that you will apply in practice.

A major point that the authors have frequently noted is that each person is different and it is imperative to be cognizant of the unique needs of the person you wish to visit. This is an important concept to keep in mind as regards all of our interpersonal relationships. What one person considers an act of kindness might be an irritation to another. Learn to be sensitive to the individual needs of the specific person you are dealing with. When in doubt, ask. ("Would you prefer that I ... or would you prefer that I not?")

I am highly impressed by the authors' thorough exploration of the topic. A careful study of this work will give the reader a deeper perspective on the importance of visiting people who are ill, and insights into how to be of real help in many ways. I am certain that this book will motivate much *chesed*.

I would like to suggest that every community start a system to facilitate *bikur cholim*. There should be a telephone number that people who wish to visit but do not know whom can call for up-to-date information on who would appreciate a visit. Someone who is ill and wishes to have visitors could also dial that number. The person in charge would have a list of volunteers who could be contacted when the need arises.

May the Almighty grant a speedy recovery to all who need it.

Rabbi Zelig Pliskin
Director of Aish HaTorah Counseling Center
Author of *Love Your Neighbor* and *Gateway to Happiness*

Acknowledgments

We would like to express our gratitude to Rabbi Moshe Chalkowski and his wife, Rochel (Bambi), whose genuine interest in and ongoing encouragement during this project never diminished, despite the many delays in completion, and who provided many valuable suggestions. Our thanks to Rebbetzin Leah Feldman for her thoughtful comments, which added sensitivity to these pages. Our appreciation to Rebbetzin Dinah Weinberg for her critique and encouragement. We are deeply grateful to Rabbi Zelig Pliskin for his review of the initial manuscript; his book *Love Your Neighbor* provided the sources for much of the material presented. Our thanks to Nahama Consuelo Nahmoud, whose enthusiasm motivated us to expand our ideas. We want to express our appreciation to Yehudit Ben Sassoon and Amalya Oren of Shaare Zedek Medical Center for assisting us with our research. We also want to thank our friends: Yehudis Sander and Yehudit Amrani, for their professional and personal advice and helpful comments; Pnina Weinberg, for her ideas and suggestions; and Nechama Berg, for her generous support and help in typing the early copies. Our deep appreciation to Rabbi Simcha Wasserman for a careful and time-consuming analysis. We also want to thank HaGaon Rav Chaim Pinchus Scheinberg, Rabbi Yisrael Altusky and Rabbi Herschel Pincus for clarifying the halachic aspects for us. Our heartfelt thanks to Tzvia Ehrlich-Klein, who gave so willingly of her time and enthusiasm to assist us with editing and proofreading, as well as offering many valuable suggestions. We are most grateful to the Lombard family and to Devorah Freimark for helping us complete this project. We want to thank our husbands, Gedaliah Shofnos and Aryeh Zwebner, who have always assisted and supported all of our efforts. And our thanks to the Shofnos children, Malka Yehudis and Baruch Zev, whose births postponed our date of publication, but provided us with additional hospital experience to write about! Lastly, we want to thank all the people who shared their stories and experiences with us to provide material for this book.

Any comments and suggestions from readers regarding this topic will be most welcome.

Introduction

Being sick, whether at home or in the hospital, is clearly a stressful experience. Depending on the severity of the illness, it can be either an inconvenience or a crisis. In any event, it can affect many people in addition to the patient.

We have all known someone who has been in a hospital, or we have been patients in a ward ourselves. Visiting the sick should be a simple matter. Yet many people actually do not visit their sick friends and relatives because it makes them feel uncomfortable. They do not know what to say, how to say it—even what *not* to say.

These feelings are understandable, particularly because people who are ill are often much more sensitive and more easily upset than usual by anything said or even implied by well-meaning friends and family. It is the *visitor's* responsibility to be aware of the sick person's hypersensitivity.

> *A woman who was hospitalized after having a miscarriage toward the end of her fifth pregnancy was told: "Chaya, it's not so bad. At least you have four healthy children at home."*

Though the woman *intended* to comfort her friend, she was insensitive to the fact that having other children doesn't mitigate the pain and loss felt after a miscarriage.

According to Rav Yitzchak Hutner, *zt"l*, the English translation of the word *bikur* in the term *bikur cholim* is not "visit" but "investigation," as in the word *bikkoret*. Our responsibility in this *mitzvah* is to investigate the condition of the sick person in order to extend *any type of help* that is needed.[1]

We know that good intentions are important and are always recognized by the Almighty. We also know that there are specific *halachot* involved in doing *mitzvot* which enable us to carry out the will of *HaShem*. *Bikur cholim* is more than a "nice thing to do"; it is a *mitzvah*, a commandment sent to us from Above. If we bear this in mind, our visits to the sick cannot help but be affected.

> *A volunteer at Hadassah Hospital was walking down the main hall when a man ran after her, anxious to speak to her. "I want to thank you for all the help you've given my wife," he told her.*
>
> *The volunteer smiled and replied, "I want to thank you for giving me the opportunity to do a mitzvah!"*

Our objective in writing this book is to enable people to put their good intentions to practical use, the goal being to provide guidelines for fulfilling the *mitzvah* of *bikur cholim* with all one's heart and ability. Since we are not halachic authorities, specific questions should be directed to a competent rabbi. Likewise, any medical questions must be referred to the proper medical authority.

The ideas and information compiled in this book were culled from professional experience in working with patients, from patients themselves, from parents and relatives of patients, and, perhaps most important of all, from being patients ourselves. All of the stories here are authentic, and they are not isolated examples, but common situations. Names and details have been changed.

Since our personal experiences were the main motivation for writing this book, the attitudes expressed here toward illness and hospitalization are those of Western culture. People from *Eidot HaMizrach* do not necessarily share these attitudes, and, in many cases, theirs may be the exact opposite of those expressed here. For example, many hospital personnel, when admitting a Sephardic woman about to give birth, have had to deal with the arrival of the woman's husband, parents, grandparents, siblings and children—who all expect to remain with the patient! Their hospitalizations are often family affairs, and visiting includes everyone, every day, for the duration of the illness. Speaking openly about illness and pain is accepted, perhaps even expected, and all family members actively share in the feelings, opinions and decisions. In such cases, not visiting the patient because "he already has too many visitors" could create hard feelings and could be insulting, as if the person "did not care enough to bother." When in doubt about a particular case, it's best to inquire regarding the patient's *minhagim* and try to make appropriate choices, keeping in mind cultural factors, practical considerations and hospital regulations. Many people in a room can disturb other patients and interfere with hospital personnel who are attending to patients, yet cultural factors should be considered, too.

We sincerely hope this book will heighten awareness of the *mitzvot* and challenges involved in visiting the sick, and thus enable all of us to fulfill our potential in doing *avodat HaShem*.

While our personal situations are very different, we recognize one thing that we have in common—the help, support and love given to us by many people and, most of all, by *HaShem*. This is what has helped us thus far and continues to provide us with the encouragement and will to live our lives to their fullest potential. For this, our gratitude to the Almighty is unlimited.

Chana Shofnos, O.T.R. (nee Helaine Willner)
Bat Tova Zwebner (nee Barbara Tatel)
Jerusalem, 1989

The Mitzvah of Bikur Cholim

The *mitzvah* of *chesed* is one of the three pillars upon which the world stands.[2] The Mishnah states that there are certain *mitzvot* for which no limit is prescribed, and man is free to decide the extent to which he will involve himself in them. One of these is *chesed*, the practice of kindness.[3] It is also stated that man enjoys the fruits of these *mitzvot* in *this* world, while the principal awaits him in the World to Come. *Bikur cholim* is specified as one of these acts.[4] There is no greater way of emulating *HaShem*, Whose *chesed* is revealed extensively in the Torah, than by doing *chesed* ourselves.

We learn something more about *chesed* from a verse in *Michah*: "Oh, man, what is good, and what does God require of you but to act justly, to love *chesed*, and to walk humbly with your God?"[5]

Interestingly, the Chofetz Chaim points out that the verse doesn't say to *do chesed*, but rather to *love chesed*. Rabbi Zelig Pliskin, elaborating on this explanation of the Chofetz Chaim, says: "We must seek ways to aid others. We should not have the attitude that we will help someone only after we are approached and, thus, cannot refuse. Rather, we should be on the alert to practice *chesed* whenever possible. A person who loves *chesed* cherishes the opportunity to help others to do *chesed* as well."[6]

Our example in emulating God in His *chesed* is clearly seen in the source of the *mitzvah* of *bikur cholim*. After Avraham's circumcision, "The Lord appeared to him by the groves of Mamre...."[7] The Talmud notes that *HaShem* appeared to Avraham on the third day following his circumcision because suffering is greatest on the third day after an operation. Just as God "appeared to," i.e., "visited," Avraham, so must we also visit the sick.[8] "Even though everything is dependent on God's will, we must do our part to aid a sick person and alleviate his suffering by visiting, etc. If we do so, it is considered as if we have saved his life."[9]

A mother was visiting her fifteen-year-old son in a hospital isolation ward after he had contracted the crippling disease of polio. He was paralyzed from his neck down, and his fever was dangerously high. The doctors feared that if he went into a coma from the high fever, he might never awaken. In order to keep him awake, the mother talked to her son about the things he enjoyed the most—sports. She discussed with him all the sports he followed, the baseball players he knew, their batting averages, home runs, World Series scores, etc. She did not stop talking for three full hours, until his fever finally broke and his recovery began.

Here we can clearly see how this mother's efforts indeed contributed to saving her son's life.

The *mitzvah* of *bikur cholim* is just one aspect of *chesed*, but one that can be performed in many ways. "*Chazal* have pointed out that *chesed* can be done with one's person as well as with his money. The *chesed* performed with one's person can be divided into three types: deeds, words, and thoughts."[10] The *mitzvah* of *bikur cholim* encompasses all three types, allowing *everyone* to participate in this *chesed*. Deeds include visiting or helping the patient; words can encourage or cheer a patient; and thoughts involve *davening* for a patient.

People often think they must understand all the details of a person's illness in order to be of help to him. We know that *HaShem* gives everyone his share of tests in His world, and we can never fully understand what another person goes through. Suffering is a very individual experience. No matter how much someone understands another person's medical problem, he still cannot judge what it means for the sick person. Nonetheless, what the Torah requires of us is to feel and act as if the other person's suffering were our own.

Rabbi Shalom Shwadron frequently relates the following incident to illustrate how differently a person will react when he really feels someone's suffering:

A little boy was playing in front of Rabbi Shwadron's house in Jerusalem. The child fell and received a nasty cut. Hearing the child's cries, Rabbi Shwadron ran outside, put a towel over the cut, and rushed with the boy to the home of a doctor who lived nearby. As he was running, an elderly lady noticed his concern and distress and, thinking it was one of Rabbi Shwadron's children, called out, "Don't worry, don't worry. God will help."

It so happened that the boy was the woman's grandson. Rabbi Shwadron was curious to see her reaction when she realized the child's identity. Sure enough, as soon as she realized that it was her own grandson, she stopped saying "don't worry" and started screaming at the top of her lungs, "My Meir! My Meir!" while neighbors tried to calm her down.

When someone else's child is involved, you might detachedly say, "Don't worry"; but when your own child is involved, you'll shout.[11]

This degree of compassion goes beyond sympathy or feeling badly for someone else; it is a complete empathy that comes from understanding people and their feelings, not just their medical problems.

A woman asked a good friend to go with her for medical treatment that she felt would be very difficult to face alone. The friend replied, "I think you should be able to handle this by yourself; if not, take one of your young children with you."

The patient realized that her friend, who always ran to do a mitzvah, might have hoped in this way to build her confidence. Still, she was hurt.

"You have a right to say you can't go with me, or don't want to go," the patient told her friend later, "but please don't judge my emotional stability. It took a lot for me to ask you to accompany me, and if I felt I could have gone alone, I wouldn't have asked."

The woman now understood the patient's feelings and how she had unintentionally erred. They have remained friends.

The Chazon Ish offers us an insight into how to acquire this ability to really feel another's suffering: "[One] first must train himself to do everything he can to save [others] from suffering. These actions will affect his emotions. Also, he should pray for the welfare of others, even if at first he does not feel their anguish."[12]

We hope that the reader will find the suggestions in the following chapters valuable. A person's goal should be to fulfill this *mitzvah* with increased sensitivity, thus maximizing the benefit for the sick person. Consequently, we will all merit greater reward for ourselves and for the Jewish people.

The Privacy of Illness

In order to help a sick person, to *daven* for him, and to give him encouragement, one need not be familiar with all the details of his illness, e.g., the name of the disease, what type of treatment is prescribed, how long it takes, results of tests, etc. The patient may not know all the facts, or may not want to disclose all this information.

When a person is in the hospital, to a great degree he is not in control of what will be happening to him. He is subjected to constant examinations by medical personnel who probe every part of his body. He may have to undergo tests of all kinds, some of them embarrassing, uncomfortable, or painful. He is questioned in detail about his life history, whether or not he feels it is relevant. A sick person often feels that he has been stripped of all privacy, and worse, that he has lost all sense of dignity. By respecting a patient's privacy, one enables the sick person to maintain his dignity as a human being, as a Jew, created in the image of God.

This is something *every* visitor can do, and it should be kept in mind when performing the *mitzvah* of *bikur cholim*.

Discussing a patient's condition can sometimes lead to unforseen consequences. Bear in mind that facts can be blown out of proportion or changed, and misinterpretations can occur.

> *A friend of mine was injured in a terrorist bus attack in Jerusalem. I called the hospital to find out how he was, and they told me he was in critical condition. Two days later I went to see him and they told me, "He's not here now." Assuming that he was dead, I was in shock at the terrible news, until I learned from his wife that he was already home!*

*   *   *

> *Once, when a visitor asked to see his cousin's new baby he was shown an infant with severe birth defects. Quite shaken up, he finally found the courage to discuss it with the mother, who firmly reassured him that he had been shown the wrong baby, who happened to have the same last name as hers!*

One must also consider how a listener will receive certain news. A woman had just given birth when her husband found out that her brother had been killed. He wanted to name their son after the brother, and had to consult a *rav* as to how to break this news to his wife. Another woman heard the news that her friend in a distant city had a serious illness, and that others were *davening* for her because she only had two months to live. Not only was this shocking, but the prognosis wasn't even true!

Finally, news can also get back to people who the patient does not want to know. In sum, one should exercise extreme caution when discussing a person's ailments, both with the patient and with others!

Prayer

*Even if a razor-sharp sword
hangs over a man's neck, let
him not despair of mercy.*

(Berachot 10a)

Praying for the recovery of someone ill is a major
aspect of *bikur cholim*. The Beit Yosef writes that one has
not fulfilled the *mitzvah* of visiting the sick if he has not
prayed for the person's recovery.[13]

The following is customarily said to the sick person:
HaMakom yirachem alecha bitoch cholei Yisrael—"May the
Allpresent have mercy upon you among the sick ones of
Israel."[14] On *Shabbat*, the greeting is: *Shabbat hi miliz'ok,
u'refuah k'rovah lavoh, v'rachamav m'rubim, v'shivtu
b'shalom*—"It is *Shabbat* and thus it is forbidden to cry
out. But recovery will come speedily, for His mercies are
many. Have a peaceful *Shabbat*."[15]

The Chofetz Chaim notes that one may pray in any
language in the presence of a sick person, since he is

addressing his words directly to the *Shechinah*, which is with the patient. However, when not in the patient's presence one should use only Hebrew, since "angels have to bear his prayers aloft, and they understand no other language."[16]

The Magen Avraham cites the *Shulchan Aruch*:[17] "One who *davens* for his friend need not mention the friend's name if the prayer is made in his presence."

In the eighth blessing of the *Shemoneh Esrei*, "*Refa'einu HaShem*" (Heal us, *HaShem*), after the words *lechol makoteinu* (all our ailments) we can add the following prayer, inserting the names of those people we want to *daven* for: "May it be Your will, *HaShem*, my God and the God of my forefathers, that You quickly send a complete recovery from Heaven, recovery of the spirit and recovery of the body, to the patient [patient's name], son/daughter of [patient's mother's name], among the other ill of Israel."

According to HaGaon Rav Chaim Pinchus Scheinberg, *rosh yeshiva* of Yeshiva Torah Ohr, Jerusalem, if the Hebrew name of the patient is unknown one can still pray for him using his English name, until finding out the Hebrew one. Other halachic authorities, however, disagree with this ruling. If there is no Hebrew name at all, one should help the patient get one. (A name can be given by making a *mi she'berach* using the Hebrew name of the patient's choice.) If the patient is unable to choose his own name, check with a *rav* on how to obtain one. If the name of the patient's mother is unknown, the father's Hebrew name may be used. If this is also unknown, one may say *"ben/bat* [son/daughter of] Sarah." If the Hebrew and English names of the sick person are both unknown, one cannot pray for this person individually (unless, as noted above, one is *davening* in the *presence* of the patient). He is, however, included in the general prayers for the sick people of *klal Yisrael*.

If someone's relative is ill, one should ask a righteous person to pray for his recovery. One should make certain he tells him when the person feels better.

> *A man once came to Rav Baruch Ber Leibowitz, zt"l, and asked him to pray for the recovery of his wife. Ten years later, Rav Baruch met that person and asked about his wife's welfare. The man answered his inquiry, and then found out that throughout the entire ten years Rav Baruch had not stopped praying for his wife's well-being.*[18]

Saying *Tehillim* is one important means of helping a sick person. Specific *Tehillim* that are recited to hasten recovery from illness include chapters 6, 9, 13, 16, 17, 18, 20, 22, 23, 28, 30, 31, 32, 37, 38, 39, 41, 49, 55, 56, 69, 86, 88, 89, 90, 91, 102, 103, 104, 107, 116, 118, 142, 143, and 148.

One may also spell out the Hebrew name of the patient by reciting verses that begin with the letters of his name. Psalm 119 is customarily used for this purpose because it consists of twenty-two sets of eight verses, arranged alphabetically. The verses in each set all begin with the same Hebrew letter. If, for example, the sick person's name is Yaakov, first say the eight verses (73-

80) that begin with the letter *yud*, then those beginning with the letters *ayin, kuf,* and *beit.* Some go on following the same pattern to spell out *bat* or *ben* (son or daughter) and the name of the patient's mother. Following this, the words *kerah Satan* (*kuf, resh, ayin, sin, tet, nun*), "Tear away Satan," are spelled out by the same method of reciting the eight verses that correspond to the respective letters.

The Purpose of Visiting the Sick

If we understand the purpose of our visit, we can fulfill this *mitzvah* in the most complete way. Remember: *We are there for the patient.* Unfortunately, when people visit the sick, they often do what *they* think needs to be said and done, rather than what the *patient* actually wants or needs. One visitor, upon entering the dark hospital room of a friend, commented on how depressing it was and began to pull up the shades, not realizing that bright sunlight disturbed his sick friend.

> *Two Jerusalem rabbis visiting a critically ill patient demonstrated this idea of providing what the patient needs. The first rabbi functioned as a go-between for the patient's family in America and the doctors in Israel. He also brought the patient his mail regularly, cheered him up, and, after the patient died, helped with the funeral arrangements. The second rabbi would enter the room and sit quietly by the patient's bed. He spoke to him calmly, never challenging or questioning what the patient told him about his therapy or his doctors.*

The patient once spoke of these visits: "I feel so honored that this rav comes to see me. Since I've come to Israel, I've gone to his shiurim [classes] twice a week, but I'm only one of many there. It's so kind of him to take the time and trouble to come and just sit by my bed without bombarding me with medical advice."

Before visiting, ask yourself honestly why you are going. Are you going to cheer up the patient and offer some company? Are you going to help out, for example, by taking the patient for tests, bringing him items from home, helping to care for him in a physical way, etc.?

These will all be elaborated upon in the following section. Of course, we must always keep in mind that we are doing a *mitzvah,* but knowing *what* we can do and are *willing* to do—and what needs to be done— makes all the difference in our visit.

Pre-Visit Considerations

Are Visitors Allowed—and Wanted?

For many people, hearing that someone is sick immediately evokes a desire to visit him. Such genuine feelings are praiseworthy, yet one should first investigate the situation before spontaneously showing up at his bedside. The would-be visitor must inquire about two things: are visitors allowed and are visitors wanted?

Visitors may not be allowed if the patient is in isolation or intensive care. A patient in isolation may be contagious, or his resistance may be so low that he is easily susceptible to major complications. This holds true even if the visitor "only has a slight cold."

Visitors may not be wanted, especially after surgery. Waiting at least twenty-four hours after surgery before visiting is a good general rule to follow. The patient may be in pain, uncomfortable, drowsy from medication, or just plain exhausted. He may have only enough energy to talk to a few select people. If others come, he may not have a chance to talk to the people he truly needs to speak with, or to have treatment, finish tests or get some rest.

A patient may be embarrassed if he needs physical assistance, or a bedpan, or if he has difficulty talking or swallowing. He may be self-conscious about changes in his appearance. If this is the case, sending a letter or note could provide needed encouragement and support without the attendant embarrassment.

Sometimes visitors are not wanted at a certain time, but would be appreciated when that period is over. If you were told "no visiting" initially, check back later to see if the medical situation has changed. Above all we should remember to think about what is *good* for the patient.

It's important to investigate the situation before visiting anyone. At the very least one should inquire at the nurses' desk before walking into the patient's room. You can always leave a note saying you stopped by.

> One woman had been out of the recovery room only one hour after a caesarian section when a friend greeted her: "Hi! I heard you've been here two days for observation, and since I had some free time before work, I thought I'd visit."
> The patient, in pain and having difficulty breathing, let alone talking, only wanted to rest. Yet here was her friend, who had taken two buses to see her. Obviously, had the visitor known that her friend had just been in surgery, she would not have visited at that time.

Sometimes one may not find out that a friend was in

the hospital until after he has returned home, or perhaps one could not visit for whatever reason. A phone call, note, or visit even "after the fact" is still appropriate.

When to Visit

If visitors are allowed and desired, one should find out the best time for the patient to see them. Close friends and relatives should visit someone as soon as he becomes ill; others should wait three days. If, however, the person is very ill, all who wish to visit should come immediately.[19] HaGaon Rav Chaim Pinchus Scheinberg comments that this is not necessarily our custom today and the proper action depends on the individual situation. The safest course to follow is to check with the family. "If a sick person desires company, anyone may go to see him before three days have passed, even if he is not very ill."[20]

A person who is seriously ill may not be aware that his situation is critical and the family may not want him to know. When flocks of visitors come, the patient might grow frightened and anxious, and realize that he is, indeed, quite sick. While the Torah gives us general guidelines, one must always be sensitive to the individual's particular situation, and inquire directly of the family, especially in cases of serious illness.

It is important to visit only when it is convenient and beneficial for the sick person.[21] This means neither too early nor too late (not before 9 A.M. or after 9 P.M.), not during doctors' visits or tests, and not when the patient's physical needs are being attended to,[22] when the spouse or children are visiting (their visit might be cut short by your arrival), and when it interferes with the hospital staff's routine or with the other patients. No one should visit a maternity ward when mothers are nursing their babies.

Hospital visiting hours are established for a good reason, and keeping to these hours enables the staff to follow their schedule. When people come at non-designated hours, they may keep the staff from performing their duties for the patient, or they may disturb other patients. Be especially courteous, sensitive and considerate to the hospital personnel, as well as to other patients in the same room. It's important to remember that when visitors leave, the patient remains behind and must maintain a good relationship with the staff and his fellow patients.

Visiting hours are not always the same for each ward, and they also vary from one hospital to another. Check the visiting hours in each case, especially since they can also be changed without prior notice.

There is a tremendous need for visiting the elderly in hospitals, nursing homes and especially at home. Regular visits, even short ones, can give these people something to look forward to and lift their spirits more than you can imagine.

Shabbat and Yom Tov

For a sick person, being in the hospital for *Shabbat* or

Yom Tov presents additional problems. Not only is the patient limited in his ability to perform the physical aspects of the pertinent *mitzvot* (*davening* with a *minyan*, eating in a *sukkah*, drinking wine, fasting, etc.), but he also misses the pleasure one experiences when celebrating with family and friends. Hospitals often are not within walking distance for relatives and close friends. Even though Jewish hospitals are lenient about visiting hours on *Shabbat* and festivals, they can still be lonely days for the patient. The loneliness is further magnified when others in his room have visitors coming and going all day long, and he doesn't. Thus, on these days, most sick people particularly need and appreciate visitors.

Many people do not realize the importance of visiting people on *erev Shabbat* and *erev Yom Tov*. Often a patient misses being involved in the usual busy preparations for these days, and he is already sadly anticipating a whole day (or two!) without visitors. Though family and relatives may make an extra effort to visit at these times, other people, busy with their own preparations, may not. It is thoughtful to consider this when you plan *your* visit.

One woman recalls, "I gave birth to my first child, a boy, late Thursday night. It was a difficult delivery, and I was drained emotionally as well as physically. I knew that Friday was not a likely day for people to visit, and even my husband's time would be limited, in order to get the shalom zachar, and everything else, ready. Suddenly, unexpectedly, in walked two friends with flowers and a warm 'mazel tov.' It was wonderful to see them, yet I was especially touched by the fact that they had made time on such a busy day to visit me."

Keep in mind that even a five-minute visit at the right time can mean a great deal to a patient.

Waiting for someone to visit on *motza'ei Shabbat* or *Yom Tov* can seem endless to a sick person in a hospital, who perhaps has already been alone for hours. A spouse at home with the children may not be able to visit right away, no matter how organized he or she is. Planning your visit for this time of day can give a tremendous boost to the patient's morale, as well as help his family.

There is a very great need for *bikur cholim* on *Shabbat* and *Yom Tov*, and during *Chol Hamoed* as well. A person who lives near a hospital or nursing home should always remember that many sick people would appreciate a short visit. One need not worry about carrying in areas without an *eruv*, since a friendly smile and a warm *"Shabbat Shalom"* greeting are more than enough to bring.

How Many and How Long?

The Gemara declares: "There is no limit to the number of times one should visit someone who is ill. It is meritorious to visit as often as possible as long as the visits will not be a burden to the patient." [23] In general, keep a visit short. [24] Of course, someone who has been without visitors all day might be hoping for an hour-long chat with a friend. Be sensitive to the patient's needs.

A patient who appears sleepy may not want to talk, but might want and need a visitor to be there with him. Some patients won't acknowledge how tired they really are, but may respond to an honest observation such as, "You seem tired, David. Maybe you should rest now." The patient may now feel freer to adjust to his fatigue. Remember, reassuring a patient that you can be with him without talking can be a tremendous comfort to someone who does not want to be alone. It is difficult to know exactly what is best in each case, and one must use his common sense and intuition to make the best decision.

It's advisable to try to limit the number of visitors to two, or a maximum of three, at a time. It can be difficult for a sick person to cope with a lot of people in the room. If a patient is able to walk and more than two visitors come, they might go to a lounge or lobby area to talk so as not to disturb the other patients in the room.

If a personal discussion is desired, one should wait until the other people leave.

Often, two women may want to visit a mutual friend, but are unable to do so due to children and responsibilities at home. In such cases, it is advisable for one friend to watch the second's children while she goes to the hospital for them both. This way, both friends have a share in the *mitzvah*. If the patient remains hospitalized, the two friends can take turns visiting.

Remember, if time permits, to try contacting the family before you visit to see if there is anything the patient needs or wants. Many times people are rushed to the hospital without prior planning, and many hospital stays last longer than scheduled. It has happened that a pregnant woman who is downtown shopping suddenly realizes that it is time to give birth and rushes straight to the delivery room. Bringing even the smallest item a patient needs or wants can make a tremendous difference to the person's well-being, and can save the family an extra trip.

Helpful Items to Bring

- Clothes from the patient's home, a towel, a face cloth, plastic shower slippers.
- Food—what the patient can eat, likes, and is allowed according to hospital rules.
- A *siddur*, books, magazines, a tape recorder with earphones, tapes, a radio, paper, pens, envelopes, stamps, small change, *Shabbat* candles when permitted by hospital regulations.
- *Tallit* and *tefillin*.
- Toiletries, cosmetics, shampoo, toothpaste, soap, tissues, safety pins, bath oils, a mirror, and plastic bags and cups.
- Shaving items for men.
- Flowers. Some people prefer plants to flowers that wilt. Neither are allowed in intensive care.
- Relatives of the patient can bring family photos, tapes or drawings from children, mail from home, papers and insurance forms.
- Clothes or a blanket for a new baby.

• Small gifts for patients to give their children when they visit: crayons, coloring books, note pads, stickers.

Keep in mind that visiting time should always be pleasant for the sick person. Visitors should dress neatly and look presentable. A patient feels good when he sees that others make an effort to present a pleasant appearance, and he feels respected as a person in spite of his illness.

Finally, people must remember not to visit if they themselves are sick, even with a minor illness, or if they have been exposed to an illness. A patient's resistance generally is weak, and therefore he and the other patients in his room are more susceptible to germs. The same holds true for the sick person at home. Nevertheless, one can still call or write a note to the patient (see pp. 70-71).

Considerations During the Visit

Before Entering the Room

Before approaching the patient's bedside, take note of the situation inside his room.

- Is the patient asleep? If so, leave a note mentioning when you hope to visit again. Visitors should also look for a note from the patient, who may have requested that his visitors wake him. Without the patient's request, it's best not to wake him up.

- Are doctors present? If a doctor is in the room, even with another patient, wait outside until he is finished. Doctors do not want visitors, even family, in the room when they are with patients.

- Is the spouse visiting? If so, offer to wait outside and let them have a little more time together. These private moments may be very important for the couple.

- Are there many visitors? If so, it's best to refrain from joining the crowd. While waiting, perhaps someone else, whether you know him or not, needs a visitor.

This is a tremendous *mitzvah*, especially since some people can spend days and weeks in a hospital without any visitors. This is especially true if they have a serious illness or a chronic one requiring extended hospitalization, if they have no family, or if they come from outlying districts, making it difficult for visitors to come. It only takes a friendly introduction and an offer of assistance. Nearly everyone longs to have some special attention or a kind word.

> *When my brother was in the hospital, he had a roommate from Europe who didn't speak English. My mother got permission to bring food for both her son and his roommate. This man's smile showed all the appreciation he couldn't express in words.*

• How does the patient look? Due to special equipment such as an oxygen tank, a heart monitor, nasal or esophageal tubes, and the like, his appearance could be upsetting. Weight or hair loss, bandages, or discoloration can also be distressing. Prepare yourself before entering.

If you are tremendously upset by the appearance of the patient, and if you have not been seen yet, just leave. If you have been seen, greet the patient and then make an excuse to leave ("I dropped my wallet..."). Regain your composure before returning to the room. Try not to show your shock at the patient's appearance; this can only upset him more.

Upon Entering the Room

The visitor should sit at eye-level with the patient. Eye contact is very reassuring. The eyes are the gateway to a person's *neshamah* (soul). Direct eye contact facilitates communication and conveys a feeling of honesty and caring. Since the *Shechinah* is at the level of the patient's bed, one should sit below the bed and not above the *Shechinah*.[25] If no chair is available, try to get one.

Do not sit on the patient's bed, and certainly not on another patient's bed. This is prohibited by hospital rules for health reasons.

A patient may be hazy from anesthesia or weary from tests, and might have trouble recognizing a visitor. Therefore, give your name and say something to identify yourself, such as, "Hi, I'm Rachel, your neighbor from downstairs."

Body language is important. A patient tends to feel helpless when visitors stand over him and stare as if he were a dreadful illness and not a person. Touch him if you would ordinarily do so. Don't be afraid of him. A hug, kiss, or pat on the arm conveys sympathy, compassion and understanding when words fail.

Sensitive Communication: What to Say

Always let the patient begin and direct the conversation. The essence of good relationships is good communication. One of the greatest pleasures a sick person can experience is the joy of feeling that he is understood by another person. Do not inquire about the person's condition or prognosis unless he initiates it. He may not want to discuss his condition, treatments, tests or results at all, or perhaps not with every visitor.

If the patient is silent or seems tongue-tied, one can start the conversation with something simple: how one got to the hospital, the weather, an upcoming event or holiday. When a person is in distress, his first need is to share his pain and feel that someone understands and cares about him. He must, however, be the one to initiate this. The greatest help a visitor can offer is to *be a sensitive listener!*

A model of how to be sensitive to another's situation has been created, and is known by the acronym REACH.[26]

Reflect: Before speaking, take a few seconds to arouse the same feeling in yourself that the patient is probably experiencing. Remember a time when you were in a similar situation, in pain, lonely, frightened, angry, or discouraged. Allow your expression to reflect to the patient that you know what he is feeling. For "A wicked man hardens his face, but a righteous man understands..." (*Mishlei* 21:29), and "Like water face to face, so is the heart of man to man" (*Mishlei* 27:19).

Encourage: Show willingness to hear the details of the situation if the patient wants to discuss them. Your task here is not to reassure, advise, and give *chizuk*, but only to "bear the yoke with one's fellow" (*Pirkei Avot* 6:6), thereby relieving his pain.

Accept: Accept whatever the person is feeling. Do

not tell him that he shouldn't be angry, sad, upset, jealous or afraid. Do not judge him or his feelings, or argue back. If a patient wants to cry, let him. Don't say, "Don't worry, everything will be all right," because in the present situation, everything is not all right! A patient once remarked that she was in a lot of pain and felt she needed to cry. Some people told her she was strong and had no reason to cry. Others assured her that her problem wasn't so bad. Another commented, "You're a religious woman, where's your *bitachon*?" This insensitivity made her feel worse because it implied not only that she should be coping better, but that her faith in God was not strong enough. It is normal for even the most religious person to have strong feelings in times of pain and distress. It is sometimes uncomfortable to sit helplessly by, watching someone cry. But a patient who feels secure enough to let out these strong feelings in front of someone else undoubtedly needs to do so, and is more likely to feel better afterwards.

Choices/Changes: This section is really for the family and close friends of the patient. Think twice before you assume you fit into this category. If a patient has not gotten the relief he wanted from sharing his feelings, then this is the point when close friends, family or *rabbanim* can encourage him to either solve the problem or adopt a positive attitude toward it. But even they must be careful not to minimize his pain. Giving people advice and solutions too quickly prevents them from using painful experiences to develop their own insights and gain confidence in their own abilities to see things more clearly. Ask what would help to decrease his anger, or what practical measures would improve his situation. This is also a good time to acknowledge the patient's strengths and abilities and point out positive aspects of his difficult predicament. This helps to restore a patient's control and maintain his dignity.

Hold/Hug: Show appreciation to the patient for having trusted you enough to share what is most precious to a person—his innermost feelings. You can also simply say, "Thank you for sharing this with me."

Remember, not all people want to be reached or REACHed. Consider the circumstances in order to know what is appropriate. A person who is recovering from surgery without complications will have different needs than a person who is fearfully awaiting a diagnosis. While a person recovering from successful surgery may be in pain or discomfort, he is in all likelihood feeling relieved that the operation is over, and that the situation has been remedied. He knows he will be stronger each day and looks forward to resuming his activities and leaving the hospital. By contrast, a person who is seriously ill and awaiting a diagnosis is worried about his results, what his treatment will be, the length of his hospitalization, how it will affect his family, his medical bills, etc. Basically, he is afraid of the unknown. Chronic problems differ from acute crises. While chronic patients may not be experiencing the anxiety of an acute crisis, they may be very depressed about their present situation and the future. All of these factors, and more, affect how a patient relates to a visitor. Visitors must understand the importance of empathy in relating to people who are ill, and it is not a simple task. When in doubt, better to say nothing than to say the wrong thing.

Sensitive Communication: What Not to Say

Never discuss with others private conversations one has had with the patient, nor repeat any information without permission.

> *A young boy had a chronic problem, and his doctor decided to do a biopsy to check if there was a blockage in his system. Since most people associate the word "biopsy" with cancer, word got out that they were checking for that disease. This eventually got back to the child, who was terrified at such news. Misconceptions about medical terms is a problem, but reinforcing these misconceptions is obviously much worse! Privacy must be respected in all situations.*

Don't challenge the patient: "Are you sure that's the test they did?" "Ultrasound is not always accurate." "It's not that bad. They probably don't know what they're talking about." Even if a person claims he broke his arm and he is lying with his leg in a cast, visitors should refrain from contradicting him. A challenging-type conversation can cause anxiety, anger or insecurity.

One should avoid disturbing and unnecessary comments. The stories patients have told of insensitive comments from their visitors are nothing short of incredible. People with serious illnesses are often asked, "How long do you have to live?" Even professionals need to be reminded what is appropriate and what isn't.

> *A man, whose wife had cancer and was due to undergo a serious operation, happened to meet a health professional from another hospital. She asked him if he had made cemetery arrangements yet! Baruch HaShem, four years later the wife was still alive and well, but the husband never got over those thoughtless words.*

*   *   *

> *A woman who was scheduled for a tubal ligation immediately after the birth of her sixth child was quite upset by the decision to perform surgery. Through her tears she heard the doctors discussing her case and the cause of her crying: "I think she has PPD [post-partum depression]...."*

This woman had a good reason to cry: she'd never have any more children. There was absolutely no need to have such a discussion in front of an obviously upset patient.

One visitor told another, "This patient is *very* sick," in a voice loud enough for the patient to hear. Ignorance is no excuse for disturbing comments and questions. If you can't say anything nice or encouraging, don't say anything at all!

It should be mentioned that too many women have been questioned unnecessarily by "friends" and even acquaintances about the circumstances surrounding their miscarriages. Questions regarding birth control, motivations for having more children, emotional problems interfering with conception, and the like are totally out of place unless the patient initiates this conversation, indicating a desire to discuss it. This follows whether the patient is in the hospital with a difficult pregnancy, has given birth, or is at home after a miscarriage or stillbirth.

Very often people do not know what to say and thus unintentionally say the wrong thing; then they avoid visiting their friends for weeks after the incident occurred. For example, a woman visiting a neighbor who had a miscarriage learned that the fetus had been deformed, and she blurted out, "The baby is better off dead."

Even if you believe this, saying it to a person after a loss does not provide comfort! This is a time to acknowledge feelings. You might say, "It must be very hard for you," or "It must be so painful," or "I can't imagine the pain you're in, Sarah, but I want you to know that I really feel for you now."

Guilt feelings are very common and are often triggered or intensified by people making insensitive comments. Feelings of shame or guilt at the time of a loss are overwhelming. But don't ignore the issue when you visit. You can simply ask, "Is there anything I can do to help?"

Giving Advice

Giving advice, in most cases, is detrimental. Before offering it, be aware that you may not have all the information necessary, nor do you have all the answers. Ask yourself these questions:

• Do you know all the facts of the illness?

• Are you sure your "good advice" applies to the person and his situation? The patient may be allergic to the very treatment you insist is most effective! Visitors may urge a patient to go to a particular institution or hospital, yet these places often only specialize in certain diseases and admit only certain kinds of patients. Unless all the facts are known, visitors should not try to persuade patients to change their hospital or treatment.

• Has this advice been given to the person a dozen times already? People often stop listening to advice they've heard many times before.

• Is the patient in the proper frame of mind to hear the advice? Offering advice on becoming pregnant is inappropriate to a woman who has just had a miscarriage.

If well-meaning advice is given, the friendship or relationship with the patient should remain the same whether the advice is followed or not.

It has been suggested that of most advice given, 30 percent is not useful, 60 percent is repetitious, and 5 percent is downright dangerous. (Recommendations of vitamins and health food diets are part of this 5 percent. Many people think that even if vitamins can't help, they can't hurt. This is not true: they can accelerate or even nullify the effect of medication.) By this estimate, only 5 percent of all advice given is actually helpful! The biggest danger in hearing too much advice is that it confuses the patient as to which treatment and doctor to follow. The patient may become nervous: perhaps he did the wrong thing. This is a tremendous emotional strain that can actually weaken a person.

Though we know that all healing comes from *HaShem,* negative comments about a patient's doctor can undermine his faith in his medical treatment. Visitors who have had bad experiences with the patient's doctor should keep their opinions to themselves! There is no benefit at this point in mentioning it to the patient, who has already made his decision and placed his trust in his physician. A patient's recovery can sometimes depend on his confidence in his doctor and the treatment that has been prescribed. A heart surgeon once said that he tries to spend as much time as possible with a patient and his family *before* surgery, because a patient who has a positive attitude has a better chance of a more complete and speedy recovery. The opposite is also true. If a patient does not have confidence in his doctor or the recommended treatment, it can hinder his recovery regardless of the help he receives. The problem can be so severe that he may refuse treatment or medication or take the latter as friends prescribe and cause himself more harm than good.

If a situation arises in which the visitor, out of serious concern, feels that the patient should switch doctors or hospitals, he should speak not to the patient but to the appropriate people (rabbis, family members, medical personnel) who can evaluate all the facts and information before making a decision. Only then should someone be selected to discuss this information with the patient. The gravity of this cannot be emphasized enough!

How should advice be offered? Avoid blanket statements and never-fail remedies. Don't force your advice on anyone; don't put someone in the uncomfortable position of having to refuse your counsel.

Wrong way: "If you do this exercise, your leg will get better much faster." Or: "When I broke my leg, I did this exercise and from my experience, I know what works."

Right way: "When I broke my leg, I did this exercise. Maybe it could help you. Perhaps you could check with your doctor and ask him what he would advise."

Giving "Spiritual" Advice

All visitors (including rabbinical representatives) must be cautious and sensitive toward the patient before offering help in the form of *mussar*. Correlating illness to specific sins or guilt is not within our realm of knowledge and must be avoided by all visitors.

> *A woman with a certain skin disease was told blatantly that she was afflicted because she had spoken lashon hara.*

*　　　　　*　　　　　*

> *While fixing some electrical equipment, a man badly burned his hands. A visiting acquaintance asked the man's wife if her husband put on tefillin every day. The wife, taken aback, replied, "Why are you asking? You know my husband is a religious man."*

> The acquaintance answered, "Well, he must not have done the mitzvah properly; that's why his hands were burned."

Efforts geared to spiritual improvement *can* help a situation. A patient who feels totally helpless may welcome an opportunity to do something for himself. And, of course, a time of trouble should be a time of stock-taking and soul-searching. If the patient initiates a conversation of this nature, he may, indeed, be looking for helpful suggestions and comforting advice. Otherwise, they can seriously affect the patient, causing anger, resentment, unwarranted guilt, and depression, alienating him from others and from *HaShem*.

Any *cheshbon hanefesh* (personal accounting) in one's relationship with *HaShem* should be left in the hands of the patient or a *rav* he feels close to. If a person does give advice or *mussar* he should first *daven* for the wisdom to say the right thing at the right time, and for his words to be received positively.

"I know someone..." stories should be avoided: "I know someone who had this disease and she's okay," or "*nebach*, she died." Even if a woman has had ten easy births, why should she have horror stories in the back of her mind when she is laboring with her eleventh? People generally tell stories to make the patient feel that he is not alone in his situation. They want to be encouraging and to let him know that others have survived the same illness. While it is true that some patients do find comfort in hearing these examples, it can often be a very delicate point for others. People who are ill and in pain are investing an incredible amount of emotional and physical energy to get themselves through their own situation. They need people to be sensitive to *them*, not tell them what *others* did. They need support and encouragement for their own specific struggles. They need to know that they are not just another medical case, who will "pull through like the others have." One should think twice before mentioning even positive examples.

"Good" Conversation

What should the visitor talk about? Everyday life! *Simchahs*, good news, an interesting event, something new or inspiring learned, or new activities in the visitor's or his family's life are all excellent starting points. Reassuring the patient that his children look good even though they miss him, and that the home is being taken care of, can be very comforting to a parent. It's very hard to be separated from family, even for a short time, and any honest reassurance given to the patient in this area is welcomed and appreciated.

Again, sensitivity is the keynote. Note the difference in how visitors tried to comfort a woman separated from her family during a hospital stay:

Wrong way: "Don't worry, your family is being taken care of. They don't need you." Or: "Don't worry, they don't even realize that you're not there." These comments were made with good intentions, yet they made the patient feel alone and unwanted.

Right way: "Your family is being taken care of. Of course they miss you, but they are waiting for you to get well and be rested before you come home." This made the patient feel more at ease, and yet wanted and needed. It also gave her an incentive to get well.

Men often appreciate someone coming to learn with them or to offer *divrei Torah* (assuming their condition permits this). Men are less likely to visit someone they aren't close to, because they feel they have nothing to talk about, yet this kind of sharing is very meaningful. Other *mitzvot* that male visitors can assist with include blowing the shofar, reading the *megillah*, buying the *arbah minim*, and helping the patient to put on *tefillin* (in case of a patient's extended stay, several men can arrange a system in which each comes on a different day of the week to help), light Chanukah candles, and shake the *lulav* and *etrog*.

A visitor should speak in a pleasant, confident manner. Lack of confidence implies fear, and overconfidence conveys denial of the illness. "Ask open-ended questions," Dr. William Fisher of Hospice, Inc., in New Haven, Connecticut, advises.[27] "Feeling better today?" shows a bias, as it suggests that the patient *should* feel better, and is a *kvetch* (complainer) if he doesn't. "How are you?" on the other hand allows the patient to respond in whichever way he wishes.

Visitors unsure of what to say might blurt out, "Hey, you look great!" when, in truth, the patient looks terrible. Don't lie. The patient knows the truth, and saying such things shows the visitor's inability to relate to him and his needs. It creates a feeling of distance between people, and interferes with honest communication.

People who are sick feel alone, separate and different from the rest of the world. This alienation is very real and can penetrate the depths of a person's being. Denying an illness by means of false communication increases this alienation, and in a sense denies the patient himself. If this happens, one loses all means of comforting and helping a patient. Of course, one need not emphasize to a patient how bad he looks just to be honest. One can acknowledge reality in a human way: "Rifki, you know you look pale, but you sound good!" Honest communication is the means to fulfill the *mitzvah* of helping a sick person feel better.

> *A woman was scheduled for a surgical biopsy. She was terrified of the procedure and, of course, quite anxious about the results. The head nurse on the ward reassured her: "We know you're frightened. None of us likes surgery. I want you to know that we're here now when you need us, and we'll be here when you come back." And they were. The nurse's kind words validated that patient's feelings, and told her that her fears were normal. Knowing that the staff was supportive enabled her to cope with her anxiety, and feel reassured that she would get the care she needed.*

Offering Concrete Help

If possible, the visitor should offer the patient some assistance.

• Does he need a message delivered, or a phone call made?

• Does he want something from the gift shop?

• Would he like to be accompanied for a treatment or test? Hospitals are generally large, and going from one section to another can be tiring, even if a patient is able to walk. Waiting for an x-ray or test can be lonely and depressing for someone who is ill, in pain, tired, or emotionally upset. Keeping him company can be comforting and meaningful. Arranging this in advance will put the patient at ease emotionally, especially if he is scheduled for an extensive clinical workup.

• Would he like to take a walk down the corridor? Often, bedridden patients would be better off getting up and moving around, but are reluctant to do so. Encouraging them emotionally and physically can be exactly what the person needs most. The patient is the best judge as to how far he can walk. Due to his condition, a sick person often has to walk much slower than his usual pace. He may feel uncomfortable about this, especially when he knows his visitor is slowing down to walk with him. The visitor may also feel awkward if he senses the patient's discomfort. If this happens, a visitor could simply reassure the patient by saying, "We'll just go slowly, David. We have plenty of time," or, if appropriate, make a light joke: "We're not breaking any track records today, take your time...." Remember, a walk in one direction requires a return trip.

• Would he like to go to the bathroom? Offer to guard the bathroom door, since locking a door is unsafe if an emergency occurs, and is not recommended for patients.

● Would he like to be read to, or to have a letter written for him?

● Would he like his pillows fluffed up, the lights turned on or off, the curtains open or shut, the bed-stand closer, the bed rolled up or down?

● Does he need help with personal hygiene (cutting nails and shampooing hair can be especially difficult) or with meals? Offer to bring tissues, or water in a cup for washing.

How Long to Stay

The length of the visit depends upon the patient's condition, the visiting hours, and the other visitors present.

It's essential to be sensitive to the patient's fatigue level, meal times, baby's nursing times, and appointments. It's best to leave on a cheerful note and not to stay too long. When leaving, one can say the customary *tefillah* (see p. 29).

Visiting the Sick at Home

Most of the suggestions for hospital visits given in the previous sections apply when visiting the sick at home. In addition, the following are a few more considerations to keep in mind.

When to Visit

The major difference between home and hospital is the lack of set hours for visiting. However, there are specific times when visiting is best. One must be sensitive to the family's needs as well as those of the patient. Children coming home from school want to see their sick parent. This is *their* time to visit. Children need quality time alone with their parent, even in cheerful situations such as a mother coming home with a newborn baby! How much more do they need a parent's companionship when sickness and pain are involved. It is essential that the parent talk with them or play with them whenever he or she is able. Before visiting, call first and check the home schedule to insure that your visit does not occur when children need attention, at mealtime or bedtime, or after school.

What to Do

Visitors should not comment on the condition of the house! One may wonder if it is proper to clean the house without asking the sick person. There is no one answer, and much will depend upon the relationship and the patient's need at the time. Many people will not ask outright for help, and some who really want it will refuse it out of shame, pride or a misplaced sense of etiquette. Some women prefer less talking and more help so that the house will look decent; others will forfeit a clean house for a warm conversation. If the visitor is able to help, it is kind to offer. But visitors should not feel that they must "take over" for a sick person at home.

When entering the house, greet the other family members, especially the children. They are having a hard enough time and need encouragement, too. Acknowledgment makes them feel appreciated. Bringing a little "busy gift" for the children (a coloring book, etc.) might also be a good idea. If there is nursing or cleaning help in the house, greet them as well.

Be careful when speaking in front of family members, including parents, grandparents, and especially children. Discussing or revealing any information is not advisable unless the listeners also know it and are willing to talk about it openly.

When a Parent is Ill

Children need special support if they are worried about a parent. They don't always understand or let others know how they feel, and they can become frightened very easily. Children often interpret conversations they overhear according to their own limited understanding and life experiences, reading a totally new and unintended meaning into the words. They also can make associations that are grossly incorrect. A child may hear that his mother is going to have a caesarian section and may visualize a baby being cut out like a painful splinter. Or he may hear that his father went to the hospital for a broken leg, and, remembering that his grandfather died in that hospital, become fearful that his father will never return.

Because a child's world is so egocentric, he may blame himself for his parent's illness, or feel that it's a punishment for his own behavior. *Never* discuss the child's behavior in connection with the parent's illness, e.g., "Your father went to the hospital; you must stop being so bad."

A child may hear part of a conversation and form his own conclusions. Children can and do misconstrue many things they hear. Never underestimate this. Parents should clarify between themselves what to tell the children, and all adults must exercise the utmost caution in speaking in their presence.

It is a comfort to an anxious child, as well as appropriate *chinuch*, to assure him that he can *daven* to *HaShem* for a *refuah sheleimah*. But be aware that illness and/or loss is bewildering for a child. A child also needs to have his feelings acknowledged, and to be reassured that the future will still be secure for him. You could say, "It is sad that Aba is in the hospital but Ima will still be here to take care of you." Or "I'm sure you feel very bad that Ima is sick, but Aba will make your snack and you'll still be able to go to kindergarten tomorrow."

Lengthy and Chronic Illnesses

A person who returns home after a hospital stay usually has plenty of visitors in the beginning. However, if there is a lengthy recovery period, the frequency of visits often decreases, though the *mitzvah* of *bikur cholim* really should be practiced on a continuing basis. Though it is usually preferable to visit in person, making a phone call or sending a letter or card can also lift the patient's spirits. Organizing a *minyan* for him is always appreciated. Unfortunately, the need for companionship is often overlooked when a person is housebound for a long time.

Even if one has not been hospitalized, living with a chronic illness requires an emotional strength that needs reviving periodically, and visits from caring individuals do just that. Many chronic conditions go into a period of remission, and the person appears to have fully recovered. Be sensitive to the fact that just because you see your neighbor out walking, at a *shiur*, or shopping, it doesn't necessarily mean that the problem or pain has gone away. It just may be in remission, or perhaps he's having a "good" day. You have no idea how difficult it may have been for him to go out for that walk, or what was really involved in getting to a *shiur*. Ask how he feels and call periodically. Genuine concern means a lot in all types of relationships.

But remember, asking means you are willing to listen to the answer! There is nothing more disheartening for a person than to share his feelings or worries about his problems with someone who really is not interested or who has no time for sensitive conversation. A person often asks, "How are you?" as a casual greeting or to be polite, and is not always prepared for the detailed answer he may receive. If you know you are unable to listen, for whatever reason, or you don't have the time to converse, you might simply say, "Gee, Leah, it's so nice to see you getting out again," or "You look good, Chaim. I'm glad you're back in *shiur*." If you'd really like to talk more at another time you can always add, "Let's be in touch next week," or "I'll call you tomorrow...." Sincere communication lets a person feel your genuine concern for him.

Don't forget that a sick person living in an outlying area is less likely to have visitors than someone in an easily accessible community. Making an extra effort to visit such a person is a tremendous *chesed* that will be greatly appreciated. A person who is sick and alone will want to spend longer periods of time with a visitor than someone who, in addition to being sick, is also busy with family concerns.

Visitors should not bring children with them, especially if they will be bothersome or make the patient uncomfortable, or if they have been exposed to illness. Inquire before showing up with possibly unwanted guests.

Visitors should create a pleasant atmosphere. If you are depressed or know you might be easily upset by the appearance of the patient, do not visit; call or send a card instead.

Phoning or Writing the Sick

According to HaGaon Rav Moshe Feinstein, zt"l, it is preferable to visit someone who is ill in person, but if this is not possible, one should at least try to telephone.[28]

A phone call expresses care and concern. It's advisable not to call too early or too late (before 9 A.M. or after 9 P.M.) or at hours when children usually need attention. Callers should start and end the conversation with good news. Avoid discussing anything serious on the phone, because one cannot see the sick person and judge how he is responding.

Some general rules for callers: Begin by identifying yourself, let the patient start and direct the conversation, refrain from asking a lot of questions, avoid challenging conversation, be wary of giving advice, and do not talk too long, as the patient might be getting tired.

Sending Notes

Letters can cheer a person up when visiting is impossible. Receiving mail can be one of the highlights of the day for one who is housebound for a long time. Keep in mind that you can't see the sick person's facial expression, and that his mood or condition may have changed since you last communicated with him. Notes should always be cheerful: "Good news...," "Wish I could be there...," "Miss you." Enclosing a picture can also mean a lot.

Besides writing good news, one could also put in "fillers," such as news clippings, cartoons, pressed flowers, or perfumed hankies. Writers can exchange recipes or information on a shared hobby. They can also encourage the person to write back by enclosing blank paper, a self-addressed, stamped envelope, and a note saying, "Hoping to hear from you soon." Perhaps the sick person could be encouraged to start a new hobby, such as collecting stamps or picture postcards, or writing to other housebound patients.

Many government agencies in the United States offer free or inexpensive pamphlets on most any topic of public interest—environment, health care, travel, home projects—upon request. A gift such as a subscription to a favorite magazine or book club is most appreciated by someone who is housebound.

Other Ways of Helping the Sick

- Shopping is very helpful, both to the housebound and to the family of a hospitalized person. This includes buying groceries; clothes and schoolbooks for the patient's children; and women's items (many husbands feel awkward purchasing these).
- Paying bills, picking up medicine, getting insurance forms, doing banking, and making important phone calls are a big help. These jobs are time-consuming and frequently nerve-wracking for the patient's spouse, who is under enough pressure.
- If a spouse is working or caring for the children, consider accompanying the patient for tests and checkups.
- Arrange for household help or a babysitter (especially *motza'ei Shabbat/Yom Tov*) so the family can go to the hospital. Make sure you know the specifics of what the family needs and wants in terms of work and the type of person to do it.
- Do whatever possible to help with small children;

knowing that the kids are taken care of eases a tremendous burden for the patient and his/her spouse. Arrange for children to get to and from buses, babysitters, and school. Let them stay in your home until a parent or older sibling returns to take care of them. Give the children lunch or supper, take them for a walk or to the park, help with homework, bathe them and prepare them for bed. If you are close with a youngster, attend his birthday party or school function if his parent cannot do so.

• If a mother is arriving with a newborn, prepare bottles, clothing and diapers. Arriving home from the hospital in any situation can be disorienting. Offering to care for children until the parent gets reorganized in the house is often very appreciated.

• Combine the *mitzvot* of *hachnasat orchim* and helping the sick: Invite the patient's children for *Shabbat* or *Yom Tov*. The decision of where to send children for a *Shabbat* or *Yom Tov* should take the feelings of the children into consideration as much as possible. Even young children have preferences. Some will only want to go to their relatives or to specific friends. Others won't mind going away at all, as long as they are kept together with their brothers and sisters. This may pose a problem, especially if the family is a large one. If one is able to offer this to a family, it can be a tremendous *chesed*, benefiting not only the children but the parents, who are spared the necessity of making separate arrangements for each of the youngsters. Keeping children together provides them with a sense of security at a time when their lives have been disrupted, when they are feeling vulnerable to change and uncertainty.

• Help with the house: wash floors, do laundry, iron (this can be done in your own home), make beds, clean the kitchen (with caution), straighten up, bring in the mail, empty the garbage. Offer to do what is realistically possible.

• Send meals for the family. Find out personal preferences, health restrictions, and which *hechsherim* are normally used. Whenever possible, send food in disposable containers, or transfer it to the patient's own pots. All food should be marked meat or dairy; if food is *pareve*, mark if it was cooked in a meat or a dairy pot. If you must send your own containers, label them with your name, address and phone number. Try to arrange to have them picked up.

• Once the patient has returned home, you might invite the entire family for *Shabbat*. This enables the patient to get out for a short while, and relieves the family of the pressure of preparing for *Shabbat*.

If your children wish to be of help in any capacity, consider the following:

• Does the patient want a child's help, rather than that of an adult?

• Is your child mature enough to handle the job? Make certain the child understands that he may call you for help, if need be. Don't coerce your child into helping, or the job will probably not be done properly, but if your child is willing, it is an excellent way of training him to do the *mitzvah* of *bikur cholim* properly.

Children in the Hospital

This section is dedicated to the memory of Chassya Sander, o"h, whose short life was an inspiration to all who knew her.

If being in the hospital is traumatic for an adult, the effect on children is almost greater than we can imagine. Bearing in mind a child's limited experience and understanding, his fears and feelings of helplessness, and his inability to adequately express these feelings, we can begin to understand how overwhelming an experience of being in the hospital can be for a youngster. This is in addition to whatever the child may be feeling about his physical condition. And this includes teenagers, who also need support and reassurance.

A child's hospitalization may result in damaging psychological and emotional consequences. The November 1979 edition of *Pediatrics*, the Journal of the American Academy of Pediatrics, noted: "When a young child must be hospitalized, the effects of the experience can be very detrimental. Several studies have indicated that these effects may evidence themselves as behavior disturbances, regressed development, retarded recovery, and the like. Two studies from Britain provide striking evidence that a hospital admission of greater than one week's duration or repeated short admissions before the age of five are associated with an increased incidence of behavior disturbances at the age of ten and into adolescence."[29]

Family, visitors and hospital staff must be sensitive and learn how to communicate with children who are in the hospital due to either accident or illness. Parents should gather information regarding the child's illness, hospital procedures, and who can help them medically, emotionally and spiritually. Visitors need to know how to relate to ill children and their families. This includes knowing what not to say, how to be supportive and helpful, and what to bring to children in the hospital. Among many other things, the hospital staff must know how to identify a child's fears and relate to him, how to respect his privacy and how to communicate sensitively with him and his family.

With this in mind we can begin to meet the psychosocial and developmental needs of our sick children.

Preparing a Child for Hospitalization

When possible and feasible, a parent should try to prepare his child for hospitalization. What and how much to say will depend on the individual situation (especially regarding how much advance notice there is), but here are a number of guidelines:

- Talk honestly but simply with your child about the medical problem.
- Explain that being in the hospital will help him get better faster.
- Explain the hospital facilities and schedules, and try to go for a "trial run."
- Discuss what toys and books to pack. (Remember to bring paper, crayons, pencils, etc.)

Some hospitals have written handouts for families regarding hospital regulations and information about specific wards, including resource people available to help families and answer questions (for example: doctors, nurses, teachers, social workers, therapists, psychologists). If not, one can inquire about all of these people, and if appropriate, arrange to meet with specific personnel, with or without the child, to prepare for the hospitalization. Ask questions like the following: What is the admission procedure? Where will my child be? Can I visit anytime? Can I stay overnight? When can my other children visit? How can I help care for my child? Can my child wear his own pajamas or clothes? What toys and clothes should I bring from home?

Take time at home to sit and talk to your child about the hospital. If he is young, have the talk a few days before admission. Children younger than four may begin to develop fantasies about the hospital and about what will happen to them if they are told too much in advance. Their sense of time is not the same as that of an adult. The older child needs more time to think about and digest what will be happening. However, you know your child best, and the timing of the talk is up to you. If you don't know the details of the actual procedure, don't guess. Information from your doctor is essential in preparing you and your child.[30]

Books of stories about children in the hospital deal with many of the issues and questions that may be on a child's mind (see Appendix). Books can open up a lot of discussion, giving the child information, and dealing with feelings, fears and misunderstandings that otherwise might be repressed. Some books portray a sick animal in the story instead of a person (children can still identify with "teddy," who wears a bandage on his head). It's best to read these books in a relaxed atmosphere, when there is plenty of time to talk to the child on his level.

As many parents know, children often misinterpret information given to them. For this reason, be doubly careful to explain everything clearly and carefully several times, asking the child to repeat to you what you have said. This may help clear up any misconceptions. For example, one child being told that she would have to be in the hospital for a broken leg thought her leg would be removed! Her mother realized this when she asked the youngster what had happened to her doll, which was missing a leg. "She has a broken leg!" answered the child.

Here are other common misconceptions held by the school-age child: during a blood test, all the child's blood may be drained away; after the application of a leg cast the leg is no longer there; the child's throat will be slit during a tonsillectomy.

Don't dismiss fantasy stories. Find out what they mean. Remember, they are very real to your child and their source could be in tales from friends, books, the media, or bits and pieces of conversations overheard from you or other family members. Always listen to your child's comments and be sensitive to his hidden fears.[31]

Be prepared for the questions your child may ask: Why am I going to the hospital? Is it my fault? Where will you be? What's going to happen to me? Will it hurt? (Don't lie. More about this later.) Will I wake up after my operation? Will I have a scar? When will I go home? Answer these questions as often as they are asked, and encourage the child to ask any others. If you do not know the answer to the question, say you will find out. After you do, tell him the answer.[32]

Information given to a child should be as simple and clear as possible. Does the child understand the vocabulary used? For example, does he know what an x-ray is? Use this as a learning experience to lessen fears, as well as to expand knowledge. Get books on x-rays, or look it up in a dictionary or encyclopedia. If possible, bring him to see the machines.

When explaining hospital procedures to your child, describe where you will be. For example, if a child will have x-rays taken, explain it like this: "The doctors want to take a photograph of your leg, so they can see the bones. It won't hurt. I'll be waiting for you right outside the door." If you're not sure whether you can be with your child during a procedure, ask your doctor or check with the hospital.

Some children are afraid that they will look different when they are released from the hospital, or that the doctor will remove something extra from their bodies. Reassure your child that an operation is only for a specific part of the body. If there will be a scar from surgery, explain how it will look. If there will be no scars or visible after-effects, make this clear as well.[33] In all discussions, try to clarify any fears or misunderstandings your child might have.

Many hospitals show children photos of the operating room, and of how the doctors and nurses will look in their green clothes, hats, and face masks. This familiarizes them with the unknown and thus decreases their fear of surgery.[34]

Another way to prepare your child for hospitalization is to play "hospital" with him, to get him to express his feelings and understand what will happen. Children can pretend to give a stuffed toy a shot, bandage a favorite doll, or make a dollhouse or cardboard box into a hospital.[35]

Upon admission to the hospital, it is most comforting for children to have some of their own belongings with them, such as familiar pajamas, a blanket, dolls, toys, etc. If possible, the child should choose what to take along. Label all belongings with the child's name. These objects help decrease the strangeness of new environments, and dolls and stuffed animals especially will help the child feel that he is not all alone. Even if the child says he doesn't need or want them, take one or two along anyway.

Taking a child on a short tour of the hospital is extremely valuable. Expectant mothers who visit hospitals to see where they will give birth can relate to how much this helps relieve anxiety. The parent should have enough information to give the child an idea of what to expect while he's in the hospital, whether it's only for an overnight observation period or for involved surgery. Tell him about tests that will be run, such as blood and urine tests or x-rays.

Keep in mind that not all of the above preparations are necessary for every child. Age and personality determine how a child relates to new experiences. Too much complex information can increase anxiety, overwhelming the child. But not enough information can keep a child in fear of the unknown. As one nurse remarked, "All new experiences are frightening to children."[36]

Hospital personnel recommend appropriate preparation for each child. Try to achieve a balance between "not enough" and "too much" information.[37] If parents remember their child's past reactions to new situations, such as the first day of school or camp, they will have a better idea of what their child needs to cope with the new and unfamiliar. Keep in mind that the ideal time to prepare a child for hospitalization is when he's young and well.

Children's Fears, Problems and Needs

As previously discussed, the newness and unfamiliarity of the hospital environment is a basic cause of fear. Peculiar tests, new people, examinations, medical equipment, plus the new routine, involving things such as morning thermometers and doctors' rounds, are all strange and somewhat frightening. All this requires an adjustment on the part of the child.

Most parents resent the impersonal attitude toward children sometimes shown by hospital staff, especially doctors. They understandably feel that this interferes with their child's adjustment. Talk to the personnel involved, before the hospitalization if possible. Many fears and anxieties can be diminished if a doctor or staff member talks to his patient kindly and respectfully, as he should to an adult. Explaining what he will do, whether it's taking blood or simply listening to his heart (and perhaps letting him listen to it as well), can reassure a youngster tremendously. Smiling at a child and being friendly before an examination only takes a moment, and can help a child feel more sure that this person cares about him and wants to help him.

Most pronounced among older children in the hospital are their fears of pain, of the knife in surgery, and of not waking up from anesthesia.[38] It wouldn't be surprising to discover that these are the major fears of adults as well! The primary fear of a child under six is separation from his parents. The school-age youngster fears bodily damage and has a hard time understanding why there is pain involved in getting well.[39]

Other fears affecting children, especially older ones, are related to body image. This is particularly true if surgery, casts, bandages, or radiation therapy causing hair loss are involved. Will their friends accept them even though they may now look different?

The child's fears regarding his illness or disability may come out in conversations with parents, but more often, because of his defense mechanisms, they will be revealed through play activities. A child may project all his problems and feelings onto a doll: "The doll is very sick. She is in pain and has to go to the hospital. She is afraid of the needle...."

Occupational therapists who work with children through play activities can often help the child work through many of these fears. In addition, the therapist will also communicate information back to the parents and hospital staff members to make them more aware of what is going on emotionally inside the child. Regarding conversations with a seriously ill child, one staff member commented, "Interestingly enough, children don't usually ask, 'Will I get better or will I die?' They just hint at it."[40]

Parents are advised to talk to the child in the here and now, for example, "You are getting well," or "You are better today," and not to talk about the future, such as, "You will get better." Though children must be given information to allay their fears, care must be taken not to destroy their hope. Regarding chronic diseases such as diabetes, or even cancer, they should be told that there are always new discoveries and new medications that can help.[41]

A child needs reassurance that no matter what happens, his parents will always love and take care of him, regardless of how he looks (with scars, amputations, hair loss, etc.). When parents are unsure of what to say, or are uncomfortable discussing such issues with their child, hospital social workers or psychologists can be most helpful. A *rebbe* or school teacher that he is particularly close with should also be made aware of the child's emotional condition before he visits or talks to him. For some children, this person may be the most important one with whom they can talk.

Other Needs

The needs of a hospitalized child are not that different from those of an adult. Depending on his age and personality, a child needs privacy. Draw the curtains when he is dressing or undressing, using a bedpan, being uncovered when attendants are making his bed, or having his hair combed. It is not unusual for a child, uncomfortable going to a strange bathroom or unwilling to use a bedpan, to refuse to call a nurse for help. Instead, he waits for a parent to come, or, in the case of a young child, he wets his bed. Patience, reassurance and privacy are needed to help the child resume appropriate behavior. Hospital personnel especially need to develop sensitivity to privacy, since it is apt to be forgotten in the hubbub of hospital routine. Exposing anyone to a lack of privacy is humiliating and degrading. Such negative feelings can remain with a person his whole life, and all efforts to avoid this should be made. Don't be hesitant or embarrassed to bring this up with hospital personnel if you feel it is necessary.

Show respect for how a child deals with his situation. Under the stress of hospitalization, his personality may change. Some children regress to an earlier stage of behavior, and this may be reflected in their play. For example, an older child may want to play in the hospital's playroom sandbox, or sleep with a doll or stuffed animal that he would never sleep with at home.[42]

The child may also regress to behavioral patterns associated with young ages, such as thumb sucking, bed soiling, nail biting or needing a bottle. Do not be critical of such regressions, or label him "childish"; understand that this is helping him cope with his situation. Even after discharge, you may see a loss of appetite, death fears, withdrawal, or whining and dependent behavior. Be understanding and accepting; remember that your child is actually expressing his fears and worries, and they should not be dismissed. You might say, "I understand lots of people feel this way sometimes." Replaying the experience will also help to work out these feelings. Within a few weeks of discharge, a child's behavior should return to normal.[43]

Being Honest

Hospital personnel and health care professionals continually remind parents *not to lie* to their sick child. If something is going to hurt, say so. The child needs to trust his parents. A child will feel deceived if a shot hurts when his parents said it wouldn't. In explaining pain, tell him that sometimes it has to hurt before it gets better, and that the pain will go away. If the child will wake up from surgery feeling sore, explain this ahead of time.

A child does not have to be told everything, but his questions must be answered. Often, short answers will suffice, for example: "There will be pain after the operation, but there will also be medication to make you feel more comfortable." A child does not have to be told the whole truth, but one must be careful in how the truth is minimized or avoided. In the above example, the child is not told that the medication will take the pain away completely, nor is he told that the pain will be very bad for the first two days. Sensitive discretion is needed.

Children don't understand why doctors, who are supposed to make them better, cause physical pain. Try to help your child grasp that things that will make him better may hurt initially or taste bad.

Reassure your child that it is all right to cry. For a child to suppress his tears can be harmful. Don't urge him to be "Ima or Aba's big boy or girl, and not a baby." If something hurts, it should be all right to cry. This is a release of tension, anger, fear and hurt. And it is healthy!

Never tell a child, "I'm not leaving," and then leave, even if he falls asleep, since you don't know when he will awaken. Don't try to sneak away. Loneliness and separation are traumatic for children. Quite apart from ethical and halachic considerations, lying to children not only decreases their trust, but increases their anxiety and fear that they will be deceived again. This can be detrimental to treatment, as well as cruel, for a child who needs rest may not be able to get it for fear that his parent will leave. If it is absolutely necessary to leave a child who is old enough to understand explanations, a note should be left, or even better, he should be told beforehand what will happen and what to expect: "Mommy has to leave for a while, but Daddy will be here till I get back." When you tell your child you will return, keep this promise. If you can't return at that time, get a message to him. Otherwise your child will wait and wait and begin to feel deserted. Expect tears when you get ready to leave. If possible, try to notify a staff member or another visitor that you are leaving, so that he can take a moment to comfort your child. Upon your return, your child may be angry with you for leaving and may react by crying or ignoring you.

Schooling and Illness

Many pediatric wards have teachers on their staff. They help children keep up with their studies (when possible and appropriate) while they are in the hospital.

A hospital teacher may have direct contact with the child's classroom teacher, and can share information as to the fears and needs of the hospitalized child.[44]

A certain child was hospitalized for kidney problems and

needed regular treatment on a dialysis machine, a lonely and time-consuming procedure, during which a child often needs company and intellectual stimulation. With the encouragement of the hospital's staff teacher, the youngster's teacher educated the class regarding this need, and then arranged visits to the child while he was having dialysis, after having gotten the approval of the child, his parents, and the hospital. Both the child and his friends benefited from the experience.

This can be an excellent means of *chinuch*, teaching the class how to do the *mitzvah* of *bikur cholim*, sensitizing children to the needs of sick people, and helping prepare an acceptable, understanding environment for the hospitalized child to return to as well. Communication between school teachers and both hospital social workers and hospital teachers is very valuable and should be encouraged. Take the initiative in mentioning this to your child's teachers, if they haven't suggested it themselves.

Visitors and Volunteers

As mentioned, loneliness in a hospital is a major cause of stress for young children. They need company, but not necessarily a lot of visitors. A young child basically needs his parents, as does an older child who is in pain, confined to bed, or in serious condition. An older child who is not in such a stressful state may need contact with friends. All children who are awake and alert and not too uncomfortable need things to do. (This will be discussed in a later section, "Visiting the Sick Child.")

A child capable of understanding needs to know that his parents may not be able to be with him all the time, that there are situations at home that need a parent's attention, and that even a parent sometimes needs a break. Furthermore, siblings, particularly young ones, require a parent's presence, even if their brother or sister is ill. If an appropriate replacement is available, the child should be told who is coming, when, and for how long. It's best if this person is someone the child knows, likes and feels comfortable with. If not, it should be someone who is comfortable and confident with children, and responsible enough to get medical help immediately in case of emergency.

A brain-damaged baby needing round-the-clock care was abandoned in the hospital. The already overburdened pediatric staff could not meet the constant needs of such a completely dependent infant. He was often left crying, unable to move, and in a soiled diaper until the staff had some extra time to tend to him. A call was put out for volunteers, and a group of teenagers was organized to care for the baby. One day, while the doctors were on their rounds, the baby went into convulsions. The fourteen-year-old girl who was caring for him immediately called the doctors for assistance. The girl's understanding and quick action brought immediate help, which otherwise would have arrived too late.

The teenagers helped care for this baby (who has since made significant progress, baruch HaShem) until foster parents were found. Here we see the mitzvah of bikur cholim performed to the fullest degree, in the purest sense.

Volunteers are often available to help. If such a service is needed, check with a community *chesed* group or with the volunteer services at the hospital.

How Parents Can Help

Dr. Robert S. Mendelsohn, associate professor of preventive medicine at the University of Illinois School of Medicine, feels it is important that parents gain skill and confidence in dealing with their child's hospitalization. Hospitals and their personnel can be intimidating, often conveying to a patient's parents the attitude of "Don't you realize *we* know what's best?" Dr. Mendelsohn makes the following suggestions to parents of hospitalized children:

> Familiarize yourself with the medication and treatment the patient is to be given. Ask about risks and side effects of drugs and treatments. Be alert to sanitation deficiencies. Don't be intimidated by doctors and nurses, or worry about being regarded as a nuisance by hospital staff. Why are parents without medical training in a prime position to meet the many health needs of their child? Simply because they are able and willing to give their child the time and attention that a doctor is not. Important elements in a hospitalized child (as well as diagnosing illness) are changes in behavior, or in appearance, and the medi-

cal history of the child. Since no one knows the child as well as the parents do, only they are sensitive enough to quickly note such in these areas. Parents are qualified to be a primary part of their child's health care, along with the hospital.[45]

This is true, however, only if the parents are coping well with the situation.

Staying in the hospital with a child round-the-clock can be very difficult for parents. In making the decision to be on constant call, a parent needs to consider the following:

• Age and personality of the child. A young child in particular wants and needs only his parents; and even an older child may not want anyone else to be with him, except perhaps a close relative.

• Condition of the child. Is he medically stable, or is he on special equipment? The more serious the condition, the more a parent needs to be there for the child's sake and for the parent's own peace of mind, but not because the hospital staff doesn't know what to do.

• Situation of family. Is it practical for a parent to be at the bedside of his sick child constantly? Perhaps there's a nursing baby at home, or the parent's own health is poor.

• Opinion of the staff. Is the parent getting very weak and physically run down? Are there emotional difficulties relating to the child and his illness, or are there discipline problems?

Parents' Problems and Needs

Any parent who has had a child in the hospital knows what a draining and stressful experience it is. The parent must deal with the cause of the child's hospitalization, and at the same time help the child to cope. The hospitalization will affect the parent's work and daily routine, and the responsibilities of caring for the rest of the family. There are also the parent's own fears of illness, disability and death to deal with. Parents need support—emotional, physical, and spiritual—in order not to feel overwhelmed by their situation.

A caring friend or neighbor can try to provide the emotional support a parent may need in facing specific challenges, such as accepting a diagnosis, coping with depression about the illness, dealing with reactions of relatives, explaining to children at home what's wrong, communicating with the child regarding his illness and treatment, and handling sibling rivalry now that most of the attention is given to the patient. Other problems that a parent faces, and that a sympathetic friend can help with, include disciplining the sick child and avoiding overindulgence out of pity for him, assuaging guilt feelings about not being able to be with the child twenty-four hours each day, coping with worries about the future, such as how to manage a chronic medical problem at home and how to help a child with a serious illness lead a normal life, and, of course, dealing with financial difficulties.[46] All of the above problems are often intensified by the parent's overall anxiety, lack of sleep, and irregular or inadequate eating habits at this time.

Though a close friend or relative is usually the most effective listener, there are also willing hospital professionals (social workers, psychologists, therapists, teachers, etc.) to help parents with these difficulties. Parents must be made to feel that there are people (rabbis, rebbetzins, close friends, relatives) who will give them spiritual support when they discuss these issues.

Families gain much comfort by knowing that others are *davening* for their child or saying *Tehillim* on a regular basis, as well as giving *tzedakah* on behalf of the patient. A family may also feel much better if a friend living in Israel goes to the *Kotel* and other holy places to *daven* for the sick child.

Various family support groups have been formed, in which problems, feelings and possible solutions are shared with others who are going through similar experiences. A friend might mention such groups to parents, which will help them realize that they are not alone in their struggle.

Many parents and professionals agree that outside help at home is a major priority when a child is in the hospital. A hospitalized child, especially a young one, needs his parents almost constantly, and they need to know that someone responsible is helping with the house and family, keeping routines running as smoothly as possible. It's best if someone can manage the entire household. If not, friends and neighbors can help by being very specific in what they can offer. For example: "Your children can come to me right after school. I'll give them lunch and they can play here until five o'clock on Monday, Wednesday and Thursday," or "I'll take your child to kindergarten and pick him up every day, and the school can call me in case of an emergency," or "I'll organize hot suppers for your family every day, including *Shabbat*, for the next two weeks." Vague offers of help are confusing to a parent and are not helpful.

The children at home need to know that they will be taken care of and who will be responsible for them. One mother felt that the best help she received came from people who knew *their own* limitations in terms of offering assistance.

When the child's condition is serious a mother will not want to leave his bedside, yet she often needs emotional support and someone to be with her as well. This should be someone she feels close to and comfortable with, in conversation, silence or tears. She also needs food and drink, and a person to relieve her when she feels she needs a break.

In other words, it should be kept in mind that *bikur cholim* is also needed for the *parent* of the hospitalized child. Even if you or your children do not know the patient you can still visit, bringing a small gift to the child and talking to the parent. One mother, whose child had a serious illness, felt that people's calling and talking to her as a person, and not just as the "parent of a sick child," really meant a lot to her. (For further suggestions, see "Other Ways of Helping the Sick," pp. 72-74)

Parents need relief both for short and long periods:

to take a walk, to eat, or to spend a few hours at home with the rest of the family. A parent keeping a watch over his sleeping child could very well use a phone call when it's most lonely. (But make certain that calling won't disturb anyone.)

"Relief people" need to be appropriate for the child as well. As mentioned they should be people the child knows and feels comfortable with, especially if they are to stand in for a substantial period.

Visiting the Sick Child

Though the primary way of helping someone with a sick child is often by providing physical, emotional and spiritual aid for him and his family, visiting the child may also be appropriate and desired by both the patient and his parents. Visitors enable the parents to have a break, keep the child from feeling alone, provide play activities to decrease boredom, offer distraction from pain and discomfort, and provide socialization through contact with friends, siblings, neighbors and peers.

There are some basic guidelines in this area of *bikur cholim* as well. A visitor should be someone the child knows, and preferably someone with whom he already has a relationship. The suggestions offered in the section on "Pre-Visit Considerations" (pp. 35-42) apply to children as well. Hospital personnel recommend that visitors tell a nurse they've arrived and ask if there is anything special they should know before seeing the child. "Most people don't do this and really should," commented one social worker.[47]

What NOT to Say and Do

A visitor should not bring food or treats to a hospitalized child before obtaining permission from the family or hospital staff. An adult who receives inappropriate food can put it in a drawer or give it away to nurses or friends. But a child with diabetes, for example, may not refuse candy, and should not even be tempted.

A visitor should not discuss the child's illness, medical condition, or treatment program in front of him or any other children. He should be made aware of what the parents have already told the child, but, when in doubt, avoid this area of conversation entirely, unless the child brings it up. If the child wants to discuss it, he should try to be a sensitive listener, without making judgments or giving advice.

A child often wants to talk about his accident, and he may be proud of his cast and may ask visitors to sign it. Another, however, may feel reluctant. A child who suffered burns because he was playing with matches, or a child hit by a car after he disobeyed his parents' warning not to play in the street, may be feeling guilty about what happened, and thus may be unwilling to discuss it.

A child who has a serious disease most often does not want to discuss it. It is emotionally painful for him, and he should not be questioned about it. Both parents and hospital staff often tell children that they do not have to answer all the questions visitors ask. This alleviates any guilt feelings the child might have about disrespecting adults or being impolite. As with an adult, one should respect the child's privacy in conversation.

What to Say and Do

Visitors should be aware that the same child they knew outside the hospital may now exhibit a different personality and behavior. As mentioned, a child often regresses in the hospital in order to deal with his difficult situation. Allow the child to play with toys *he* chooses, even though you may have just bought an expensive gift you were sure he'd adore! (More about this later.) Avoid any criticism of "childish" behavior or activities he wants to do.

Playing with children is the best thing to do when visiting, assuming this is appropriate for the child's condition. A child may not want to be fed, washed, or taken care of by visitors, but usually responds favorably to play activities or being read to.

Toys and books are the best gifts for a child in the hospital. Select a toy that is sturdy, safe, and practical for the child's medical condition. A child who has injured his dominant arm should not be brought writing or coloring activities that require the use of that arm, or even a toy that requires the use of both hands simultaneously. It is best for both parents and visitors to leave expensive toys at home for when the child returns, in order to avoid bad feelings if something gets broken or lost. Practical gifts include family photo albums, stuffed animals, dolls, puppets, card games, coloring books, crayons, colored pencils, drawing paper, puzzles, magnetic games such as checkers or chess, simple weaving projects such as loop potholders, Etch-a-Sketch, a flashlight (especially for a child who likes to read in bed), Rubik's Cubes (and other one-piece puzzles), postcards, stationery, and stickers. For an older child, consider bringing group games, or a tape recorder and cassettes. Parents are the best source of information as to what the child enjoys.

Activities Children Can Do for a Sick Friend

It is important for the child's friends to keep in touch with him.[48] A class could make a tape with short messages from each child, songs, stories, *divrei Torah*, jokes, or news of what the class is learning. They could also send drawings, postcards, stickers, crossword puzzles and word games (for older children), and even homework. If the child is in the hospital for two weeks or more, items can be sent more than once.

Don't be embarrassed to suggest this to the child's teacher as a *chesed* project. Teachers can even motivate their students to improve their writing by rewarding them for legible handwriting and neat cards. The entire class could also collaborate on a gigantic get-well card, decorated and signed by all the students.

For a housebound child, receiving mail may be the highlight of his day. Parents can help a child use the mail he receives for interesting projects: marking on a large map just where the letters came from, or putting all the *divrei Torah* received into a special notebook or onto a tape for future use. Children can also send a sick child a riddle in a letter and give the answer in the next letter. While the patient is trying to solve the riddle, he can also look forward to receiving the answer. In addition, they can send parts of puzzles in several letters, giving the child something else to look forward to.

If the sick child is reluctant to do homework in order to keep up with his class, his *rebbe* or teacher could assign something specific that a friend could learn with him during a visit. Rewards for successful learning can be offered to motivate both the patient and his friend.

Everyone appreciates receiving get-well and greeting cards, as well as a telephone call from a friend. Remember, however, that depending on how he's feeling, the child may not want to talk long, so be sure to make a young caller aware of this. Even a quick hello reminds a sick child that his friends are thinking about him, and this is worth a lot. Of course, if possible, visiting the patient after checking first with the family is ideal.

No more than two visitors should come at the same time. When more children visit, they end up playing with one another instead of giving their attention to their sick friend.

Parents should prepare young visitors for what they might see in regard to the patient (who might look different), or to other patients (who might be on special equipment, etc.). Children must be instructed about proper behavior in a hospital. When there is any doubt about whether they've gotten the message, parents should accompany children and then wait outside the room while they visit. Children can bring a game to play with their sick friend while they visit, or even something to lend him while he is in the hospital. Remember that no one should visit if he has a cold or even minor symptoms of such.

Children often remember hospital experiences their whole lives. Any effort to minimize the trauma is clearly in the realm of not only *bikur cholim*, but *ahavat Yisrael*, love of a fellow Jew.

Conclusion

How great is the *mitzvah* of *chesed*, which includes
bikur cholim? The Chofetz Chaim explains that there are
two traits with which *HaShem* conducts the world: strict
justice, and kindness and compassion. These Divine Attributes are both actually in accordance with the prin-
ciple of justice. The extent to which a man's conduct
exemplifies these traits in this world is the extent to
which he merits the corresponding traits from their
heavenly sources.[49] In other words, if a person deals
with others with compassion and kindness, then
HaShem has compassion for him—and the world—for
his sake. As *Chazal* have declared, "Everyone who has
compassion for his fellow creatures is himself granted
compassion from Heaven."[50]

Now we can appreciate why, throughout the Torah,
"*HaShem* desires lovingkindness" from His people.[51] It is
so that, in the end, He can also behave toward His
people with *rachamim* (compassion).[52]

Chesed is one of the foundations of the world, a

foundation that helps man love God by loving his fellow man, thereby transcending himself and the physical world in which he lives. It brings man close to God, the source of good, and thus, our greatest pleasure. *Chesed* gives man pleasure in this world because doing good enables him to feel good himself. How much greater will the pleasure be in the World to Come!

How great is *HaShem*, who enables us to receive pleasure in this world, while allowing us to accumulate unbounded pleasure in the World to Come! Our efforts are never in vain, for "according to the effort is the reward."[53] Rabbi Samson Raphael Hirsch explains that it is the measure of earnest striving, of devoted endeavor for the realization of good purposes, that meets with God's approval and determines the true worth of man and his life.[54] Thus, we must always remember, when trying to encourage ourselves and others to perform the *mitzvah* of *bikur cholim*, that sincere effort is what brings us merit in the eyes of the Almighty.

A Few Personal Stories

The stories patients tell can teach all of us what is meaningful to a sick person. The following are a few enlightening *bikur cholim* experiences.

*   *   *

When I was ten, I had surgery and was in the hospital for a month. Every day my mother brought me noodle soup. It was the only food I ate for a long time, and later the only food I enjoyed. She never missed a day; I'll never forget that!

*   *   *

After my first caesarian, I was in a lot of pain and I really didn't want any visitors except my immediate family and close friends. My husband (without telling me) let others know this, and I was so happy to see people when, on the fourth day, I finally felt better! Also, even the people who I know were "very busy" and came only for five minutes were great! It's amazing how wonderful a five-minute visit could make me feel once I was up to having visitors.

*   *   *

I was having out-patient treatment in the hospital daily for a number of weeks. I remember one day in particular, because in addition to the unpleasant treatment, my children were also sick at the time. The doctors kept reminding me that someone else could take care of my children while they were sick, but only I could take care of my medical problems, which were much more severe. I could not stop thinking about my sick children, and felt guilty that I was taking care of my own problems instead of theirs.

I had made arrangements for my children to be taken to their pediatrician. I returned home to hear that they had been to the doctor, and, thank God, they weren't as sick as I thought. They had even been fed, given their medicines and put to bed.

A letter had arrived from one of my closest friends, reminding me that everyone sent love and best wishes, and was davening for me. The phone calls I received from people asking how I was also helped me feel better. Knowing my children had been taken care of relieved my guilt and tension; receiving the letter and phone calls reminded me that even when I felt discouraged, others were rooting for me. The next day, when I returned to the hospital for treatment again, I was a much calmer person.

*   *   *

A stay in the hospital is a real lesson in how important

chesed is. Even if one comes armed with notebooks, aero-grams and books, the loneliness in the ward is a palpable reality. One day slowly turns into another while you spend hours weakly watching the cars speeding down the avenue outside, the clouds moseying by in the sky, and the nurse fixing your infusion bag.

The walk to the pay phone becomes the excitement of the day. Even though the nurses and other patients may kibitz with you, you are longing desperately for your husband and children, your busy schedule, and your friends. And then in walks a friend with a smile on her face. You feel like jumping out of bed in excitement, but she holds you back, "Don't get out of bed! What's new? How are you feeling?"

Well, you generally feel about 25 percent better just because she is there visiting you. But would she understand that if you'd say it, since she doesn't know how it feels? The pleasant talk makes you forget how lonely you are and you don't realize until later how energized you suddenly feel. Even after she leaves, the smile on your face doesn't disappear. This inner joy is compounded all the more when you know that in your home all is in order, due in large degree to the members of your community who are sending nutritious meals to your family and otherwise helping out.

*   *   *

When I was in the hospital, every visitor brought a ray of sunshine into each dreary day. Sometimes people would come with small gifts or reading material, which made me feel especially good. Shabbat was the hardest. The hospital was not within walking distance for anyone I knew, and being away from my husband and children was very lonely.

On top of everything else, my roommates had people coming and going all day, which made me feel uncomfortable.

One Friday afternoon, while emotionally preparing myself for the day ahead, a group of teenagers came into our room full of good cheer and small talk. They distributed a red rose and a "Shabbat Shalom" to each patient. What a nice surprise! Just having that rose next to my bed made Shabbat a little nicer.

*　　　　　*　　　　　*

My recovery after surgery was relatively uneventful. In fact, that's the point—it was painfully boring lying there in that hospital day in and day out.

Fortunately for me, once a day my first cousin came to visit me, and I received a measure of the warm, caring companionship I needed. I remember feeling disappointed that I would still be in the hospital for her birthday. Not only would I not be able to go out and celebrate with her, but I couldn't even give her anything. She was so wonderful and took such good care of me throughout this whole hospital ordeal, and now her special day was coming and what could I do to make her happy? I looked around the room and spotted a fresh hospital nightie draped over a chair. Suddenly I had an idea! After getting permission from the night nurse, I used all of my brightly colored marking pens on the white nightie, and designed the latest fashion in hospital gowns! It was quite glamorous, not to mention unusual! That night, my cousin came by unexpectedly to surprise me with all the birthday treats and *trimmings. What a celebration! But I surprised her with an exclusive designer gown attractively wrapped up in paper towels! Attached to it was the only birthday wish I could think of at the time: "You should NEVER have to use it!!!" It was the best day I had had—until the next day, when they discharged me to go home!*

*　　　*　　　*

When my oldest son was three-and-a-half years old, one of his baby brothers was scheduled for elective surgery. I tried to explain to him that his brother was going to the hospital so the doctors could close his cleft lip.

Being nervous myself, I felt that I had not given my young son the impression of confidence.

I sent a note to my son's rebbe on the day of the surgery so that he would be aware of any personality changes in my son. Late that afternoon, after the surgery, I arrived home and noticed that my son was a lot calmer than he had been in the morning, before going to cheder. I asked him what he had done that day. He described the following:

When the boys went outside to play, one rebbe went with the children and the other rebbe told my son to sit down next to him. The rebbe said he knew his brother was in the hospital and, with HaShem's help, the doctors would make him well. Then the rebbe said Tehillim. My son didn't know how to say Tehillim. His whole face lit up as he told me what he'd done instead, "My rebbe said I could say alef-beit for my brother, and I did! I helped my brother! Then the rebbe gave me pretzels and we went outside."

There is a great deal to be learned from this final

story, as we examine how the *rebbe* helped the child.

The *rebbe* served as a role model for the youngster, showing him an appropriate response to the situation— in this case, saying *Tehillim*. The child also learned that each person must do what he can, to the best of his ability: even saying *alef-beit* can be sufficient!

By letting the child *daven* for his baby brother, he was given the feeling of being an active participant in his brother's recovery. Finally, the *rebbe* let his student know he was available if the youngster wanted to talk, or if he needed him.

This *rebbe* was able to provide the emotional and spiritual support needed by his young student. This sensitivity is clearly within the realm of *bikur cholim*.

Baruch HaShem, many individuals and organizations spend their time, money and energy helping others in need. While numerous individuals are already involved, more people are always needed to help. May the Almighty continue to bless and strengthen these people in all their efforts, and may you, the reader, also become part of them.

Prayer for the Sick

[Lord, Lord, benevolent God, merciful and compassionate, slow to anger and abounding in kindness and truth. You preserve kindness for thousands of generations, forgiving iniquity, transgression, and sin, and You cleanse.]

O Lord, Yours is greatness, power, splendor, victory, and glory, for everything in Heaven and Earth is Yours. Yours is kingship, and You reign supreme over all rulers. You hold the soul of every living thing, the spirit of all mankind, and the power to strengthen and heal. Nothing is beyond You.

May it be Your will, faithful God and merciful Father, Who heals His people, Israel, tends His beloved, and redeems His pious, to cure in abundant kindness, graciousness and compassion [sick person's Hebrew name], the son/daughter of [sick person's mother's Hebrew name], lest his spirit descend to the grave. Have mercy upon him and rejuvenate him, in answer to our prayers. May his merits appear before You, and may You cast his sins into the depths. Overcome Your anger against him, and grant him a complete recovery, spiritually and physically. Renew his youth like an eagle, and grant him—and all the ailing of Israel—a cure blessed with peace and life.

Fulfill the verses transcribed by Moshe, Your trusted servant: "...if you obey the Lord, your God, and do what is proper in His eyes, heeding His commandments and observing all His decrees, then I will not strike you with any of the diseases that I brought on Egypt. For I am the Lord, your healer...."

And uphold the words of Your prophets: "And you shall eat plenty, and be satisfied, and praise the name of the Lord, your God, Who has dealt wondrously with you, and My people shall never be ashamed. I have seen his ways and I will cure him; I will guide him and console him and his mourners. I will create a new expression of the lips: Peace, peace, both far and near, says the Lord, and I will heal him. [And] for you who fear My name, the sun of righteousness shall arise with healing in its wings. Then shall your light burst forth like the dawn and your health shall swiftly blossom."

Heal us, O Lord, and we shall be healed, save us and we shall be saved, for You are our glory. Heal the wounds of Your people, Israel, especially [sick person's Hebrew name], the son/daughter of [sick person's mother's Hebrew name], and grant his 248 organs and 365 veins/all her organs and veins a complete recovery. Cure him as You cured Chizkiya, king of Yehuda, and Miriam the prophetess with Your thirteen attributes of Divine mercy.

Please, God, heal [sick person's Hebrew name], the son/daughter of [sick person's mother's Hebrew name]. Raise him up from illness and lengthen his days, that he may serve You in love and fear. Grant him a life of mercy, health, peace, and blessing, "For length of days and long life and peace shall they [the commandments] add to you." Amen Selah.

In Appreciation

Growing up with a physical disability since early childhood presented me with myriad challenges in many areas. One of the most significant of these was developing self-respect and self-worth despite being different from everyone else. The loving, supportive environment I had provided me with the opportunity to learn skills necessary for living and to accomplish and succeed in those activities for which I had the capabilities.

Difficulties are part of everyone's reality, but encouragement from others was there, every step of the way. This, I feel, is what enabled me to recognize my limitations yet focus on my abilities in order to make the best of what I had. Maintaining this perspective as an adult is no less important, nor is it any easier. The challenges change, and at times the tests seem harder. The support is what makes the difference.

I want to thank *HaShem* for giving me all that I've needed throughout my life, and for enabling me to appreciate all that I have.

I also want to thank my mother, Mrs. Etta Willner, for creating a home filled with warmth and security, and my father, Jack Willner, *o"h*, for having the emotional strength to support our family throughout the many trials and tribulations we went through.

I am deeply grateful to the Rifka Laufer *bikur cholim* organization in Brooklyn, which helped us in so many ways during a difficult trip to New York for medical reasons. I especially want to thank Mrs. Bella Brodt for making all the necessary arrangements for us, and constantly making sure that all our needs were taken care of; and Rebbetzin Rifka Weisenthal, for contacting physicians and helping us with medical appointments. A very special thank you to Avrohom and Gitty Lichtenstein and their lovely family for their warm hospitality and genuine care and concern, and for providing us with a real "home away from home."

Though my hospital experiences have continued here in Israel, *baruch HaShem* they have been for *simchas*—the births of our four children. My deepest appreciation goes to my husband, Gedaliah, whose love and encouragement has supported me throughout the births (and each of the lengthy recoveries) of our children: Yaakov Mordechai, Esther Yentl, Malka Yehudis, and Baruch Zev, who are my greatest source of *nachat*. While the *bikur cholim* organizations in Israel may not be as large or sophisticated as they are in New York, the quality of help offered by many people is indeed significant and worthy of mention. I especially want to thank my dear friend Hadassah Auerbach for organizing a network of help with the utmost care and sensitivity when I most needed it; and a personal thank you to each of the "team members" who played a tremendous part in assisting me: Zelda Pindras, Rifka Epstein, Mimi Kleinman, Shifra Slater, Elly Braun, Miriam Eisler, Miriam Marcus, Alice Katz and Chani Shapiro. I also want to thank Professor Bruno Berkowitz, who has always listened to me as a person as well as a patient.

In truth, this list could go on and on, and in light of this, I sincerely extend my appreciation to all those not mentioned who have helped me.

My final thank you goes to my friend Bat Tova Zwebner. Not only did her insights motivate me to undertake this project, but her sensitivities taught me a great deal more about the *mitzvah* of *bikur cholim*.

Chana Shofnos

In Appreciation

A few years ago I was diagnosed as having a potentially fatal illness, for which I was to undergo uncomfortable and lengthy treatment.

Though I had been taught that every person has the inner strength to cope with, and overcome, any test given to him, I never thought that I would indeed find the strength to face mine.

Even though the strength has to come from within, it's knowing that others care, and are trying to help, that gives a person the will to live and the incentive to be as active as possible.

I would like to give thanks to *HaShem* for having given me thirty-one complete years of life, and for each and every day afterwards.

I would also like to thank my family and friends, whose kind words and actions gave me encouragement, help, and hope.

In particular, I thank my husband, Aryeh, and our children, Eliyahu, Miriam, Benjamin, Baruch and Yehoshua, who have been a constant source of *nachat*. My appreciation also to my parents, Mr. and Mrs. Melvin Tatel; my in-laws, Rabbi Dov Zwebner, z"l, and Mrs. Chava Zwebner; my brothers, Harvey, Chaim and Eliyahu; my sister, Marcia; my brother-in-law, Shlomoh Chaim; my sisters-in-law, Leah and Ronna; and my nephews and nieces.

I would like to thank HaGaon Rav Moshe Stern, HaRav

Yechiel Michael Stern, Rabbi Shlomo Rokeach, and HaRav Dovid Nesher, z"l, as well as Rebbetzin Leah Feldman and Rebbetzin Tziporah Rokeach, for their spiritual guidance and practical help.

My appreciation to Professor Aharon Poliack, Dr. Joel Lafair, and Professor Bruno Berkowitz, Dr. and Mrs. Goldwag, Dr. Finkler, and the staff of Hadassah Ein Karem and *Kupat Cholim Amos* for their medical attention. Despite their busy schedules, they always made the time to give me hope and encouragement.

The list of friends and neighbors I'd like to thank would take a whole book to write, so I ask forgiveness of those I do not mention, but I want you to know I haven't forgotten.

I would like to mention Rabbi and Mrs. Yaffee, Mrs. Penny Serasik, Mrs. Miriam Fried, the Younker family, Linda Raxenberg, Gayle Jaffee, Sharon Backman, Hindy Wiseberg, and Joseph and Dina Cotton.

A special thanks to Neshe Ezrat Torah, who are busy with their own families, yet always make time to help others by sending meals, babysitting and so on.

And thank you to the girls from Beit Yaakov Seminary who, as part of their busy schedules, help with community projects.

Also, a very special thank you to Chana Shofnos for her ideas, sensitivity, and consistent efforts to finish our project.

Bat Tova (Barbara) Zwebner

Notes

1. R. Yitzchak Hutner, *Pachad Yitzchak*, Brooklyn: Gur Aryeh Institute for Advanced Jewish Scholarship, "Letters and Writings," p. 55.
2. *Mishnah Avot*, 1:2.
3. *Mishnah Peah* 1:1.
4. *Shabbat* 127a.
5. *Michah* 6:8.
6. R. Zelig Pliskin, *Love Your Neighbor* (Jerusalem: Aish HaTorah Publications, 1977), p. 21.
7. *Bereshit* 18:1.
8. *Sotah* 14a.
9. Rabbeinu Tam, *Sefer HaYashar*, ch. 13, cited in Pliskin, p. 52.
10. Chofetz Chaim, *Ahavath Chesed*, trans. Leonard Oschry (Jerusalem: Feldheim, 1976), p. 224.
11. Cited in Pliskin, pp. 129-130.
12. Chazon Ish, *Kovetz Igrot Chazon Ish*, vol. I, p. 123.
13. *Shulchan Aruch, Yoreh Deah* 335:6.
14. *Shabbat* 12b.
15. Ibid.
16. Chofetz Chaim, p. 201.
17. *Orach Chaim* 119.
18. R. Yitzchak Edelstein, *Rav Baruch Ber Leibowitz: Chayav U'pheulotav*, p. 97, cited in Pliskin, p. 55.

19. *Shulchan Aruch, Yoreh Deah* 335:1.
20. HaGaon Rav Yosef S. Eliyashuv, cited in Pliskin, p. 54.
21. *Shulchan Aruch, Yoreh Deah* 335:4.
22. Rambam, *Hilchot Aivel* 14:5.
23. *Shulchan Aruch, Yoreh Deah* 335:2.
24. *Sefer HaMidot L'HaMeiri*, p. 180.
25. Interview with HaGaon Rav Chaim Pinchus Scheinberg, Jerusalem.
26. Miriam Adahan, *Raising Children to Care* (Jerusalem: Feldheim, 1988), pp. 120-121.
27. Ruth and Arthur Schwartz, *Good Housekeeping*, March 1979.
28. HaGaon Rav Moshe Feinstein, *Igrot Moshe, Yoreh Deah* 223.
29. Robert S. Mendelsohn M.D., *How to Raise a Healthy Child in Spite of Your Doctor* (Chicago: Contemporary Books, 1984), p. 235.
30. *A Child Goes to the Hospital* (Washington: Association for the Care of Children's Health, 1987).
31. Ibid.
32. *Preparing Your Child for the Hospital—A Checklist.* (Washington: Association for the Care of Children's Health, 1987).
33. *A Child Goes to the Hospital.*
34. Interview with Amalya Oren, pediatric social worker, and Yehudit Ben Sassoon, teacher, Shaare Zedek Medical Center, Jerusalem, July 1988.
35. *Preparing Your Child for the Hospital—A Checklist.*
36. Interview with Yehudis Sander, R.N., Hadassah Hospital, Mount Scopus, Jerusalem.
37. Interview with Oren and Ben Sassoon.
38. Ibid.
39. *A Child Goes to the Hospital.*
40. Interview with Oren and Ben Sassoon.
41. Ibid.
42. Ibid.
43. *A Child Goes to the Hospital.*
44. Interview with Oren and Ben Sassoon.
45. Mendelsohn, p. 235.
46. Ben Branscomb, Hernan Moreno, and Sally Whitley Ben-

droth, "Identification and Management of Psychosocial and Environmental Problems of Children with Cancer," *American Journal of Occupational Therapy* 33, no. 11, November 1979, p. 713.

47. Interview with Oren and Ben Sassoon.
48. Catherine O'Neill, "Helping a Child in the Hospital: What Friends Can Do," *Washington Post*, 17 March 1987, health section.
49. Chofetz Chaim, p. 88.
50. *Shabbat* 151b.
51. *Michah* 7:18.
52. Chofetz Chaim, p. 89.
53. *Mishnah Avot* 5:27.
54. R. Samson Raphael Hirsch, *Chapters of the Fathers*, trans. Gertrude Hirschler (Jerusalem: Feldheim, 1979), p. 96.

Appendix

Children in the Hospital: Books for Parents

The following books are recommended by the Association for the Care of Children's Health. They may be purchased from the Association:
3615 Wisconsin Ave, N.W.
Washington, D.C. 20016
(202) 244-1801

1. *A Child Goes to the Hospital.* Suggestions for parents in preparing their child for a hospital stay. 16 pp. $.75 (book no. 56)
2. *Caring for Your Child in the Emergency Room.* Explanations of common emergency room procedures and hospital personnel, and suggestions on how parents can help their child before, during and after an emergency room visit. 16 pp. $.75 (book no. 172)
3. *Preparing Your Child for Repeated or Extended Hospitalizations.* Guidelines for self-education using support services, working with hospital staff and understanding the

emotional and developmental needs of a child with special health needs. 16 pp. $.75 (book no. 77)

4. *Special Care Babies.* A young child's experience with the hospitalization of a sibling born prematurely is described and illustrated. 23 pp. $2.95 (book no. 190)

5. *For Teenagers: Your Stay in the Hospital.* Helps acquaint adolescents with hospital routine and policies, staff and common medical terms. With annotated bibliography. $.75 (book no. 72)

6. *Caring for Your Hospitalized Baby.* Information on the effects of hospitalization on growth and development, and suggestions on how parents can help their baby in the hospital. 16 pp. $.75 (book no. 167)

A variety of high-quality children's books are available explaining the hospital experience and helping young people cope with the stresses of hospitalization. Parents of children facing imminent hospitalization would be well advised to speak to librarians for a list of helpful works. The *sefarim* store, too, with its large selection of high-quality children's works touching on themes such as *bitachon,* can be a valuable resource.

Interested readers are welcome to contact the authors for guidance and referrals in this area.

Chana Shofnos
531/4 Kiryat Kamenetz
Neve Yaakov, Israel

Bat Tov Zwebner
25/2 Ezrat Torah
Jerusalem, Israel

Hachnosas Orchim in the Hospital

The following article appeared in the October 1988 issue of the Jewish Observer. Our thanks to both the Jewish Observer and the author, Galia Berry, for permission to reprint it here.

Wearily, Asher shifted uncomfortably in the hard plastic chair. *Shabbos* had begun four hours ago, and perhaps now, after the excitement and tension had settled, he would be able to rest as best as the bright orange chair would allow. It would be a long, hard night. The weight of his heavy head was barely supported by his stiff neck. Indeed, as he dozed, he would wake up with a start as his bearded chin jerked onto his chest.

The only chair he was accustomed to on Friday night was the thickly upholstered one at the head of his *Shabbos tisch* at home. It was admittedly a bit inconvenient, having to spend the night in the orange plastic chair in the Jerusalem hospital of Misgav Ladach, but *baruch Hashem* his wife had given birth to a healthy child after *licht-bentching* time, having checked in that Friday morning. He had found a little *shtiebel* to *daven Ma'ariv*— what neighborhood in Jerusalem doesn't have a *shul* on every other block?—and then returned to the hospital, to check on his wife, now sleeping comfortably, and their beautiful newborn daughter. He was glad that his wife had thought to pack a little cake and fruit, or he wouldn't have eaten that *Shabbos* night, for he lived on the outskirts of Jerusalem, and walking home was out of the question. So it seemed that the hospital room would be his bed chamber that *Shabbos* evening. He shrugged, shifted uncomfortably, and dozed off again lightly.

*   *   *

Asher awoke to find a hand resting on his shoulder, nudging him gently. He looked up, and saw a tall, handsome *chassid*, regally dressed in a silk *bekeshe* and *streimel*.

"*Gut Shabbos*," the intruder said softly. "I am sorry to disturb your *menuchas Shabbos*," he grinned. "Perhaps I can offer you more comfortable accommodations? We live only a block away, and my wife and I are always looking forward to *Shabbos* guests! Have you eaten a proper *Shabbos* meal yet?"

Asher could only mumble that he had managed a bit of cake and fruit. But that was sufficient....

"Nonsense! You must come to us! Admittedly, we ate a few hours ago, but we have plenty of tasty leftovers!"

(The *chassid* mumbled to himself, "*Ach*, I knew I should have come immediately following *shul!*")

Interrupting himself, he added, "By the way—do you have a *Mazel Tov*? A new daughter? *Mazel Tov*! Lots of *nachas*! You know, we have a very comfortable bed for you at our home; really much better than that hard chair you're sitting on!"

Asher thought he had better check on his wife again, and was comforted to see that she was sleeping soundly. He told the nurses to inform his wife, should she awaken, that he would return the following morning.

And so, the *chassid* took Asher to his home. His name, Asher found out on the way, was "Reb Avraham Yitzchak" and he made it his custom to visit the hospital every *Shabbos* eve and morning in search of husbands who had become "trapped" in the hospital due to their wives giving birth, and then, due to distance, were unable to make their way home until *Motzaei Shabbos*. His wife "Sara," Reb Avraham Yitzchak explained, always cooked plenty of food to insure that there would be enough for the expected "unexpected" guests, in addition to having at least two beds prepared in advance for guests just like Asher.

*　　　　*　　　　*

The next morning, Asher awoke, feeling rested and happy, incredibly grateful to *Hashem* that He had given him and his wife a beautiful daughter, as well as for the *hashgacha* that had delivered him into the hands of Reb

Avraham Yitzchak and his family. He *davened* at a nearby yeshiva, and returned to the hospital so he could wish his wife *"gut Shabbos,"* make *Kiddush* for her, and gaze upon the miracle of the tiny new life in the bassinette.

Asher knocked softly on the door, expecting to find his wife asleep. *"Gut Shabbos,"* he smiled. His wife was holding their daughter, her eyes dancing and face beaming. She looked at Asher quizzically. Asher grinned, "You're not going to believe this, but...." He proceeded to tell his wife all about the wonderful *chessed* shown to him by his gracious hosts, and how he was looking forward to spending *Shabbos* lunch with them as well. This way, he could spend the rest of the day with his wife and baby, relaxed, rested and well-fed. His wife was delighted and grateful. Meanwhile, Reb Avraham Yitzchak was not idle. With two of his seven children in tow, he unobtrusively and politely went from room to room, making sure that all the patients' husbands had made arrangements for their *Shabbos seuda*. Only when satisfied that they lived nearby, or were planning to eat with friends, did he venture into the next room.

Reb Avraham Yitzchak peeked into the recovery room, which was naturally quieter than the other rooms on the busy floor. There was a lone patient there, and at her bedside sat her husband, his lined face revealing anxiety and concern. Somehow the *chassid* sensed that it would be inappropriate to initiate the conversation with his standard, *Do you have a Mazel Tov?*, for the woman appeared to be in pain.

"Excuse me, '*gut Shabbos.*' Is there anything I can do to help?"

Yosef gazed at the *chassid* in front of him, who seemed to appear from nowhere. To each side of him was a small boy and girl, peeking out shyly from behind their father's *bekeshe*.

"Perhaps you would care to join us for our *Shabbos seuda*? We live only a block away."

Yosef looked questioningly at his wife. She suddenly had terrible stomach pains, and both the doctor and the *Rav* had advised that she go immediately to the hospital, for it seemed to be a matter of *pikuach nefesh*. Yosef hadn't even had a chance to *daven* or think of his own needs. He had rushed by car to the hospital, having arrived but a half hour earlier. Tests revealed that she had internal hemorrhaging, but not all the laboratory results were in, and there was no final diagnosis as yet. Surgery seemed likely at this point—both were frightened by the prospect. Yosef had been *davenning Shachris* when the *chassid* had entered the room.

"You go, Yosef," his wife said quietly. "You haven't yet managed to eat a proper *seuda* this *Shabbos* day. We won't have any answers yet for at least another two hours. Go—you need a place to relax a bit. It is easy to forget it is *Shabbos* here!"

Yosef didn't know what to do. He hated to leave his wife, who was clearly in pain and would be very much alone. But here was a *Shabbos* angel in the guise of a *chassid* offering him a small taste of *Shabbos*, with the promise of a family *tisch*, *divrei Torah*, *cholent*....

"Are you sure it is all right if I go? I feel awful leaving you alone...."

"I insist!" said the wife, and Reb Avraham Yitzchak took Yosef's arm and escorted him out of the room. "*Refuah shleima* and *gut Shabbos!*" he called to Yosef's wife. "And if there is anything I can do to help you—perhaps you would like one of my children to stay here with you so you won't be alone?"

*　　　　*　　　　*

Yosef returned two hours later. He found his wife alone in the room, lying in bed, singing *Shabbos zemiros*. She explained, "I don't feel the pain so much when I sing and concentrate on the words. I am trying to bring *Shabbos* into the hospital room! How was your lunch?"

Yosef smiled at his wife. "*Baruch Hashem!* Such a wonderful *chessed* that man and his wife perform! Do you know that they come to the hospital every *Shabbos* in search of guests?"

Yosef seemed much more relaxed, and his new demeanor helped his wife feel calmer, too. She had an army of nurses and doctors to worry over her and care for her, but no one except Reb Avraham Yitzchak and his wife Sara had concerned themselves with her husband's feelings of distress and helplessness. For those precious two hours, they had restored to Yosef the aura and *simcha* of *Shabbos*—through their kind words, their gracious and genuine hospitality; the normalcy of lively children singing *zemiros* and spouting *divrei Torah*;

the steaming, delicious foods served from the beautifully set *Shabbos tisch*.

A week after the crisis had passed, Yosef's wife was discharged from the hospital. Asher's wife had been released a few days earlier. To their acquaintances, they related the wonderful *hachnosas orchim* by Reb Avraham Yitzchak and his wife, only to find out that their hospitality each and every *Shabbos*—no matter how inclement the weather, no matter how many the guests—was already well known. Few people who had found themselves at Misgav Ladach Hospital in Jerusalem on a *Shabbos* had not been touched by their hospitality, and everyone agreed that their *Shabbos* had been greatly enriched as a result.

Bibliography

Adahan, Miriam. *Raising Children to Care*. Jerusalem: Feldheim, 1988

Birnbaum, Philip, trans. *Daily Prayer Book (HaSiddur HaShalem)*. New York: Hebrew Publishing Co., 1949.

Branscomb, Ben; Hernan Moreno; and Salley Whitley Bendroth. "Identification and Management of Psychosocial and Environmental Problems of Children with Cancer." *American Journal of Occupational Therapy* 33, no. 11, November 1979.

Chofetz Chaim. *Ahavath Chesed*. Translated by Leonard Oschry. Jerusalem: Feldheim, 1976.

Fosson, Abe, and Elizabeth Husband. "Bibliotherapy for Hospitalized Children." *Southern Medical Journal* 177, no. 3, March 1984.

Hirsch, Rabbi Samson Raphael. *Horeb*. Translated by Dayan Dr. I. Grunfeld. London: Soncino Press, 1984.

Mendelsohn, Robert S. *How to Raise a Healthy Child in Spite of Your Doctor*. Chicago: Contemporary Books Inc. 1984.

O'Neill, Catherine. "Helping a Child in the Hospital: What Friends Can Do." *Washington Post*, 17 March 1987, health section.

Pliskin, Rabbi Zelig. *Love Your Neighbor*. Jerusalem: Aish Ha-Torah Publications, 1977.

Resources on Child Health Care. Washington: Association for the Care of Children's Health, September 1987.

Scherman, Rabbi Nosson. *The Complete Artscroll Siddur.* New York: Mesorah Publications, 1984.

Schwartz, Ruth and Arthur. *Good Housekeeping.* March 1979.

Hutner, Rav Yitzchak. *Pachad Yitzchak.* Brooklyn: Gur Aryeh Institute for Advanced Jewish Scholarship.